S0-AQK-627

DATE DUE

FEB 1 3 2009			

FOLLETT

GRAPHIC SCIENCE

EXPLORING

ECOSYSTEMS

WITH MAX AXIOM
SUPER SCIENTIST

by Agnieszka Biskup

illustrated by Tod Smith

Consultant:
Dr. Ronald Browne
Associate Professor of Elementary Education
Minnesota State Univeristy, Mankato

Capstone
press

Mankato, Minnesota

Middle School of Plainville LLC
Plainville, CT

Graphic Library is published by Capstone Press,
151 Good Counsel Drive, P.O. Box 669, Mankato, Minnesota 56002.
www.capstonepress.com

Copyright © 2007 by Capstone Press. All rights reserved.
No part of this publication may be reproduced in whole or in part, or stored in a
retrieval system, or transmitted in any form or by any means, electronic, mechanical,
photocopying, recording, or otherwise, without written permission of the publisher.
For information regarding permission, write to Capstone Press, 151 Good Counsel Drive,
P.O. Box 669, Dept. R, Mankato, Minnesota 56002.
Printed in the United States of America

1 2 3 4 5 6 12 11 10 09 08 07

Library of Congress Cataloging-in-Publication Data
Biskup, Agnieszka.
    Exploring ecosystems with Max Axiom, super scientist / by Agnieszka Biskup;
illustrated by Tod Smith.
    p. cm.—(Graphic library. Graphic science)
    Includes bibliographical references and index.
    ISBN-13: 978-0-7368-6842-6 (hardcover)
    ISBN-10: 0-7368-6842-9 (hardcover)
    ISBN-13: 978-0-7368-7894-4 (softcover pbk.)
    ISBN-10: 0-7368-7894-7 (softcover pbk.)
    1. Ecology—Juvenile literature. I. Smith, Tod, ill. II. Title.
QH541.14B57 2007
577—dc22   2006029490

Summary: In graphic novel format, follows the adventures of Max Axiom as he explains the
science behind ecosystems.

Art Director and Designer
Bob Lentz and Thomas Emery

Cover Artist
Tod Smith

Colorist
Matt Webb

Editor
Donald Lemke

Photo illustration credit: Corel, 17

TABLE OF CONTENTS

SECTION 1

COMMUNITIES OF EARTH -------- 4

SECTION 2

ENERGY FOR THE PLANET ------- 10

SECTION 3

WORLD'S BIOMES ----------------20

SECTION 4

A DELICATE BALANCE ---------- 24

More about Ecosystems and Max Axiom 28–29
Glossary 30
Read More 31
Internet Sites 31
Index.. 32

SECTION 1 COMMUNITIES OF EARTH

While trekking through a vast canyon, Super Scientist Max Axiom finds himself on an exploration into earth's ecosystems.

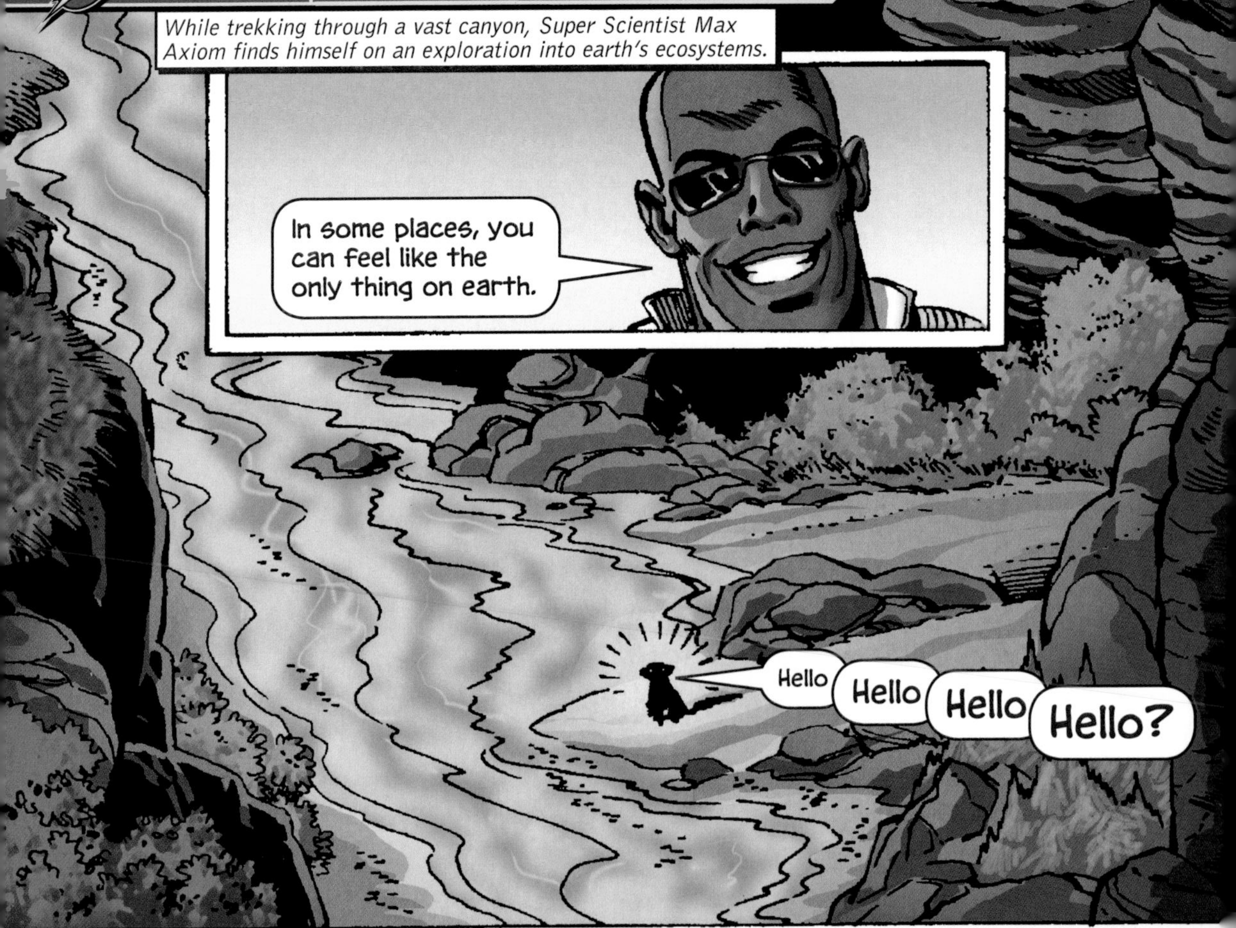

In some places, you can feel like the only thing on earth.
Hello
Hello
Hello
Hello?

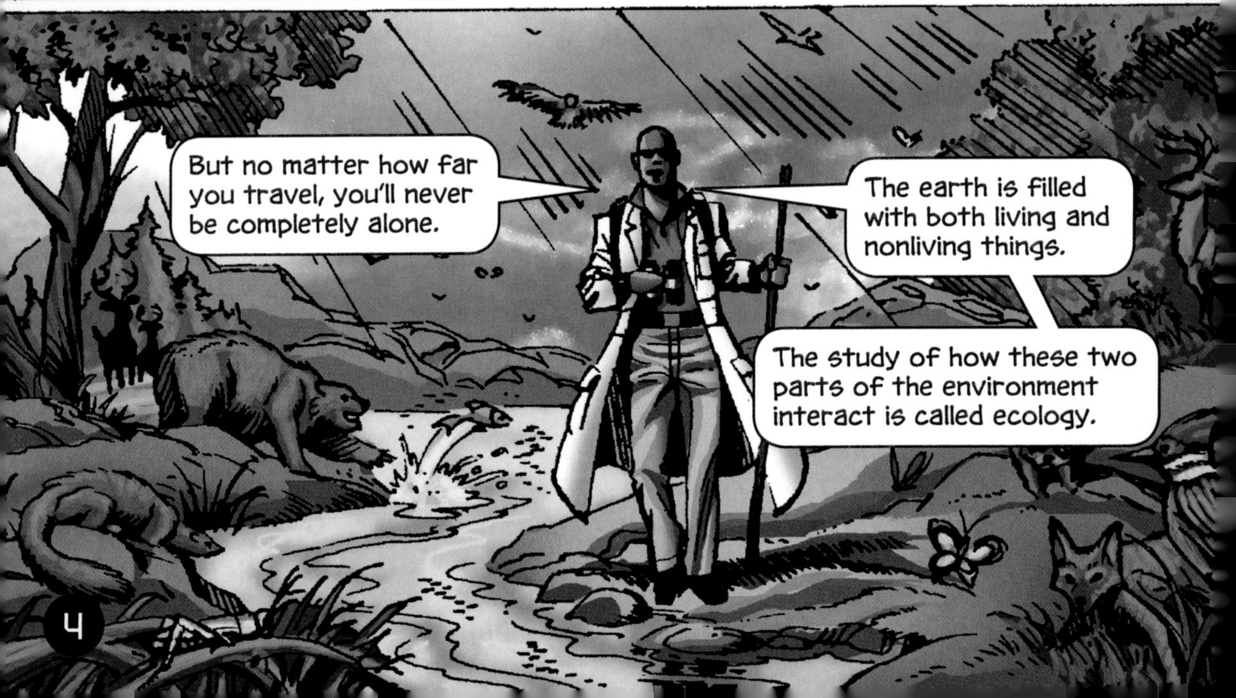

But no matter how far you travel, you'll never be completely alone.
The earth is filled with both living and nonliving things.
The study of how these two parts of the environment interact is called ecology.

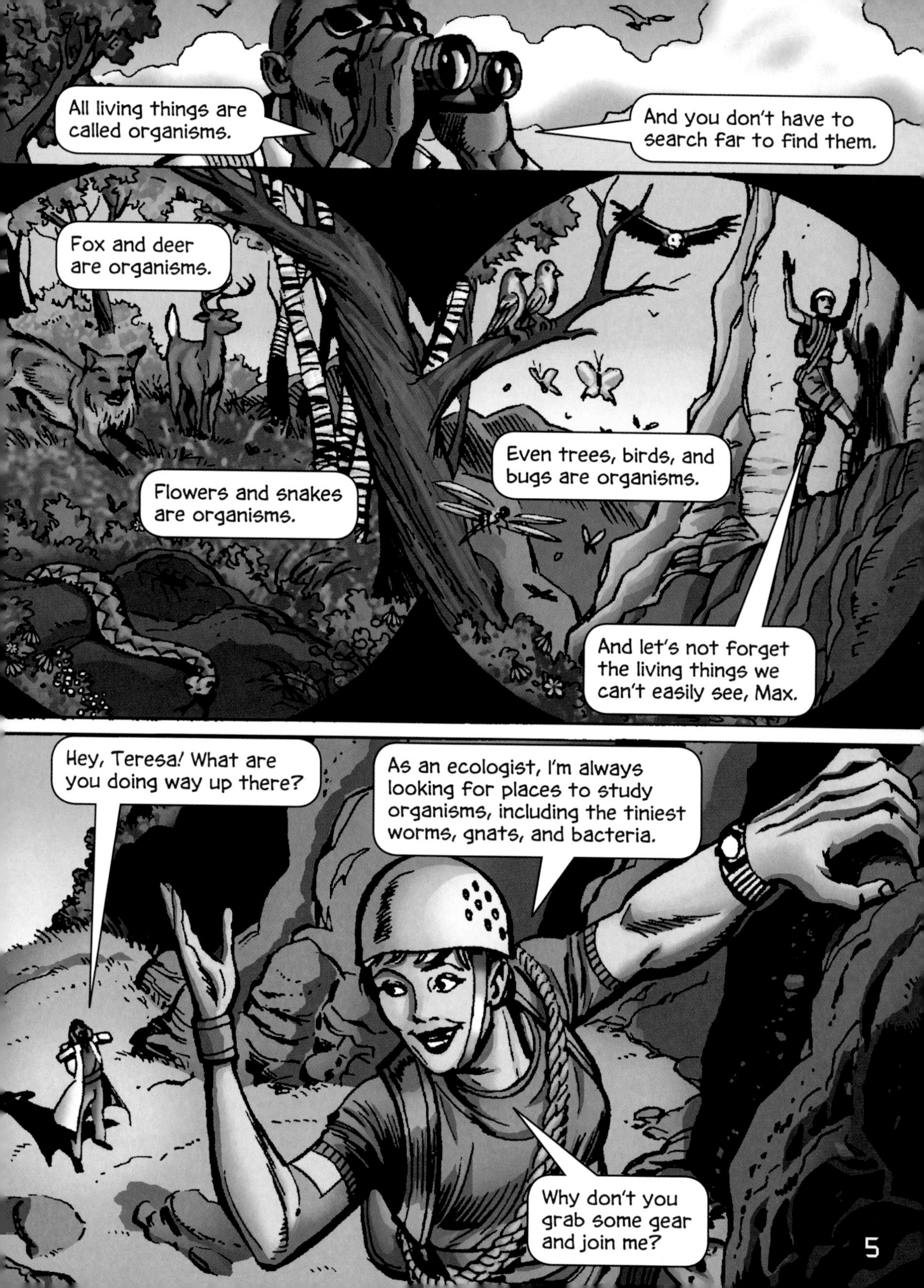
All living things are called organisms.
And you don't have to search far to find them.
Fox and deer are organisms.
Flowers and snakes are organisms.
Even trees, birds, and bugs are organisms.
And let's not forget the living things we can't easily see, Max.
Hey, Teresa! What are you doing way up there?
As an ecologist, I'm always looking for places to study organisms, including the tiniest worms, gnats, and bacteria.
Why don't you grab some gear and join me?

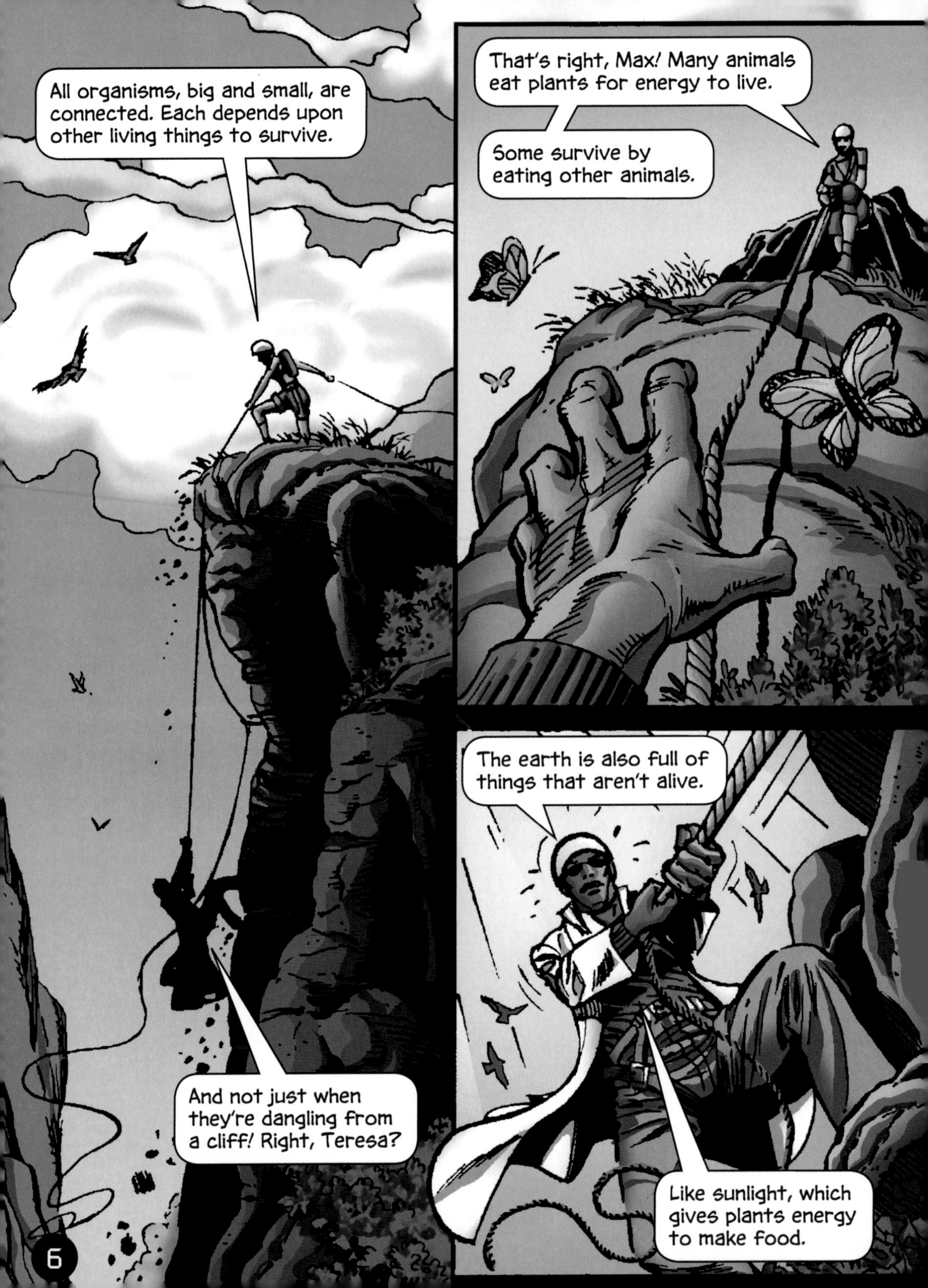
All organisms, big and small, are connected. Each depends upon other living things to survive.
And not just when they're dangling from a cliff! Right, Teresa?
That's right, Max! Many animals eat plants for energy to live.
Some survive by eating other animals.
The earth is also full of things that aren't alive.
Like sunlight, which gives plants energy to make food.

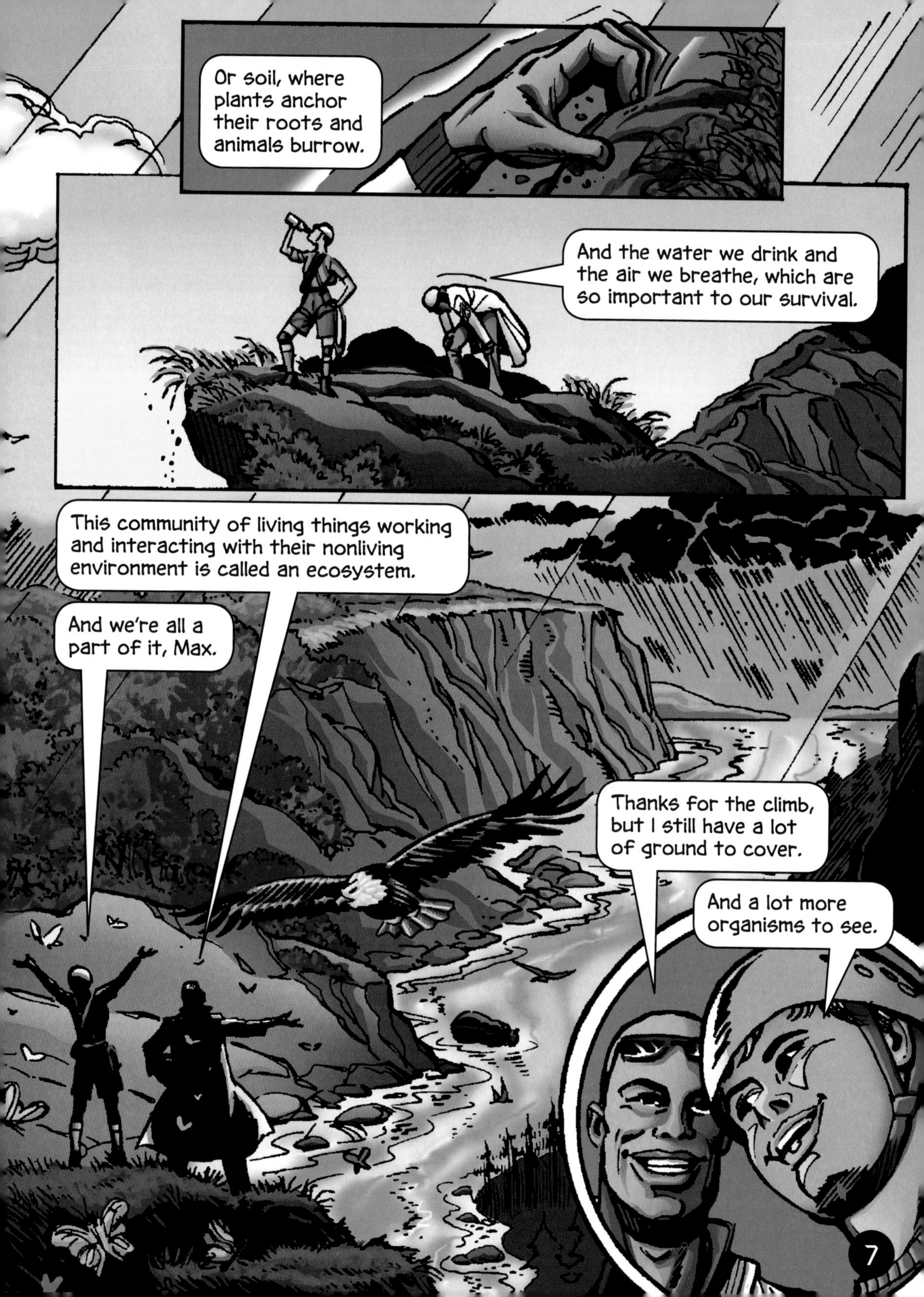
Or soil, where plants anchor their roots and animals burrow.
And the water we drink and the air we breathe, which are so important to our survival.
This community of living things working and interacting with their nonliving environment is called an ecosystem.
And we're all a part of it, Max.
Thanks for the climb, but I still have a lot of ground to cover.
And a lot more organisms to see.

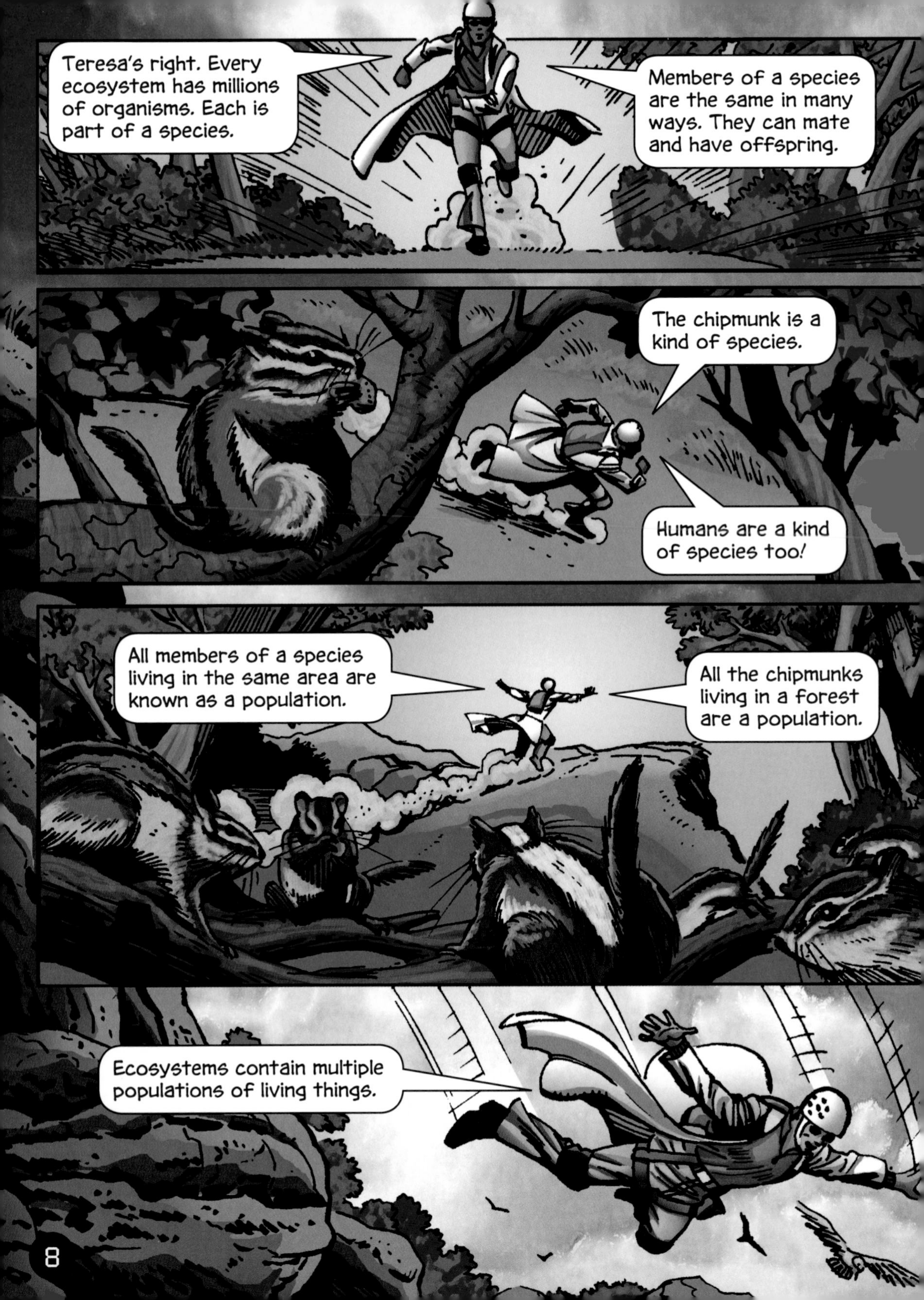
Teresa's right. Every ecosystem has millions of organisms. Each is part of a species.
Members of a species are the same in many ways. They can mate and have offspring.
The chipmunk is a kind of species.
Humans are a kind of species too!
All members of a species living in the same area are known as a population.
All the chipmunks living in a forest are a population.
Ecosystems contain multiple populations of living things.

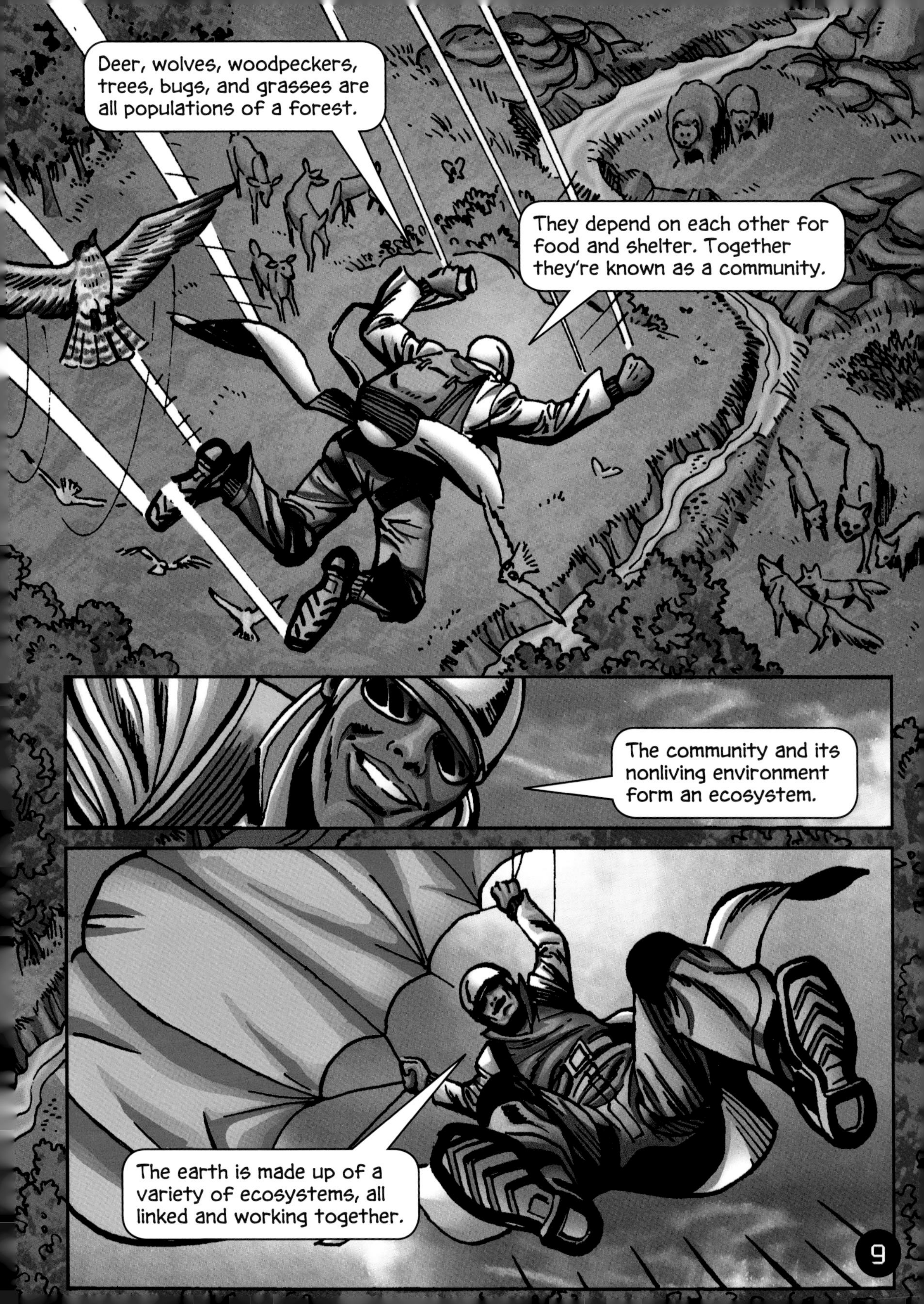

Deer, wolves, woodpeckers, trees, bugs, and grasses are all populations of a forest.
They depend on each other for food and shelter. Together they're known as a community.
The community and its nonliving environment form an ecosystem.
The earth is made up of a variety of ecosystems, all linked and working together.

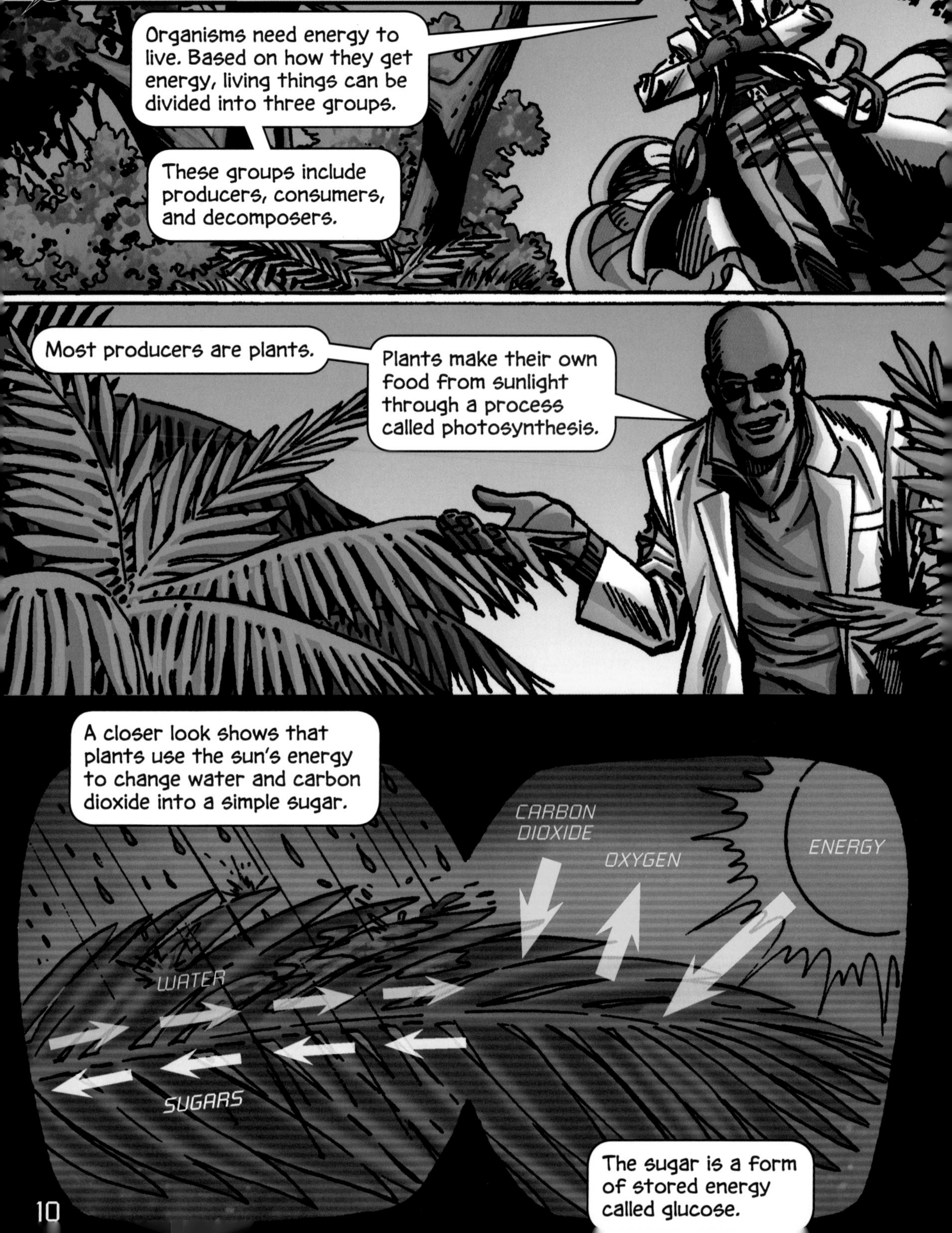
Organisms need energy to live. Based on how they get energy, living things can be divided into three groups.
These groups include producers, consumers, and decomposers.
Most producers are plants.
Plants make their own food from sunlight through a process called photosynthesis.
A closer look shows that plants use the sun's energy to change water and carbon dioxide into a simple sugar.
CARBON DIOXIDE
OXYGEN
ENERGY
WATER
SUGARS
The sugar is a form of stored energy called glucose.

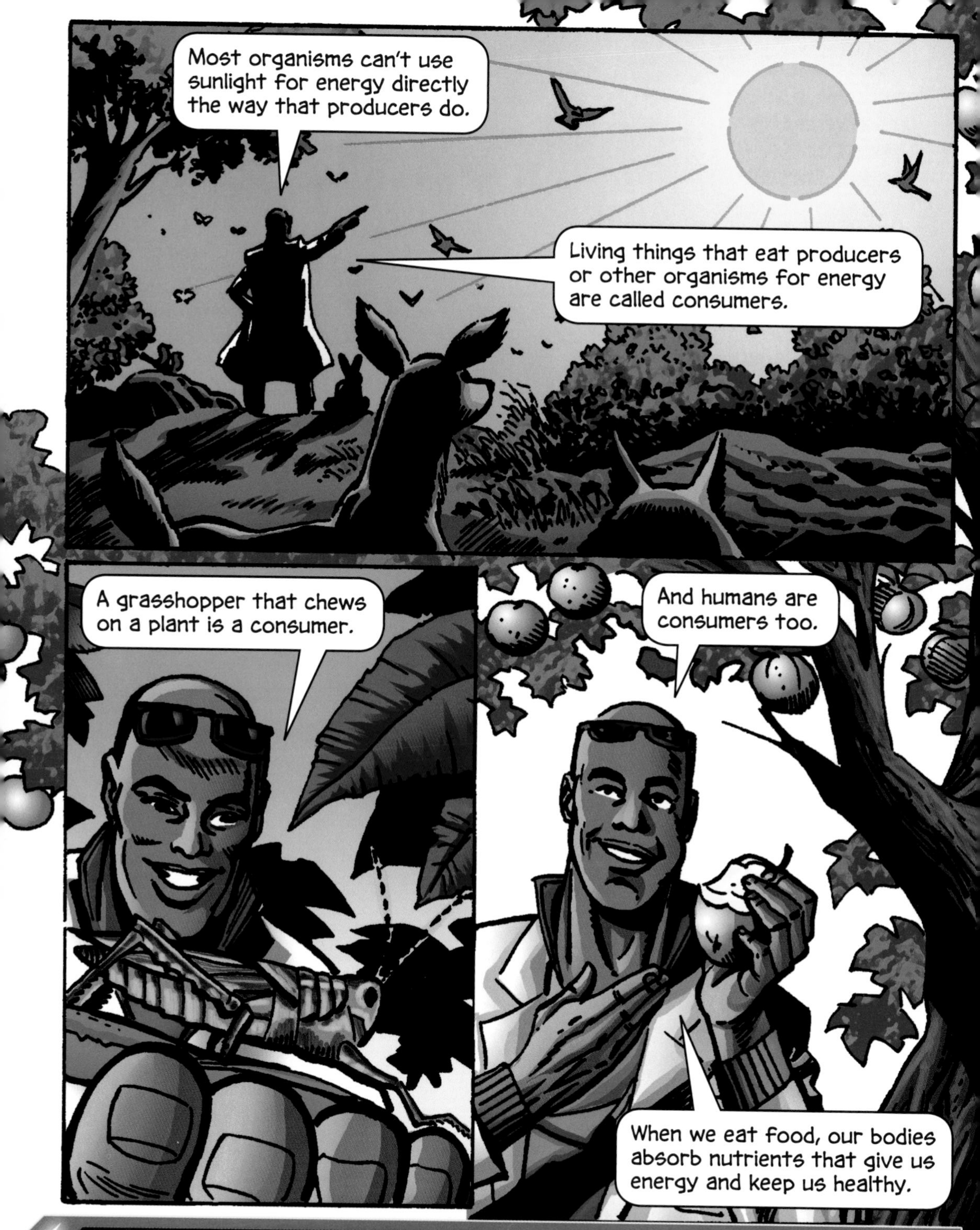
Most organisms can't use sunlight for energy directly the way that producers do.
Living things that eat producers or other organisms for energy are called consumers.
A grasshopper that chews on a plant is a consumer.
And humans are consumers too.
When we eat food, our bodies absorb nutrients that give us energy and keep us healthy.

DEFINITION

nutrient (NOO-tree-uhnt)—a substance needed by a living thing to stay healthy; plants get nutrients mainly from the soil in the form of minerals; animals get nutrients mainly from the foods they eat.

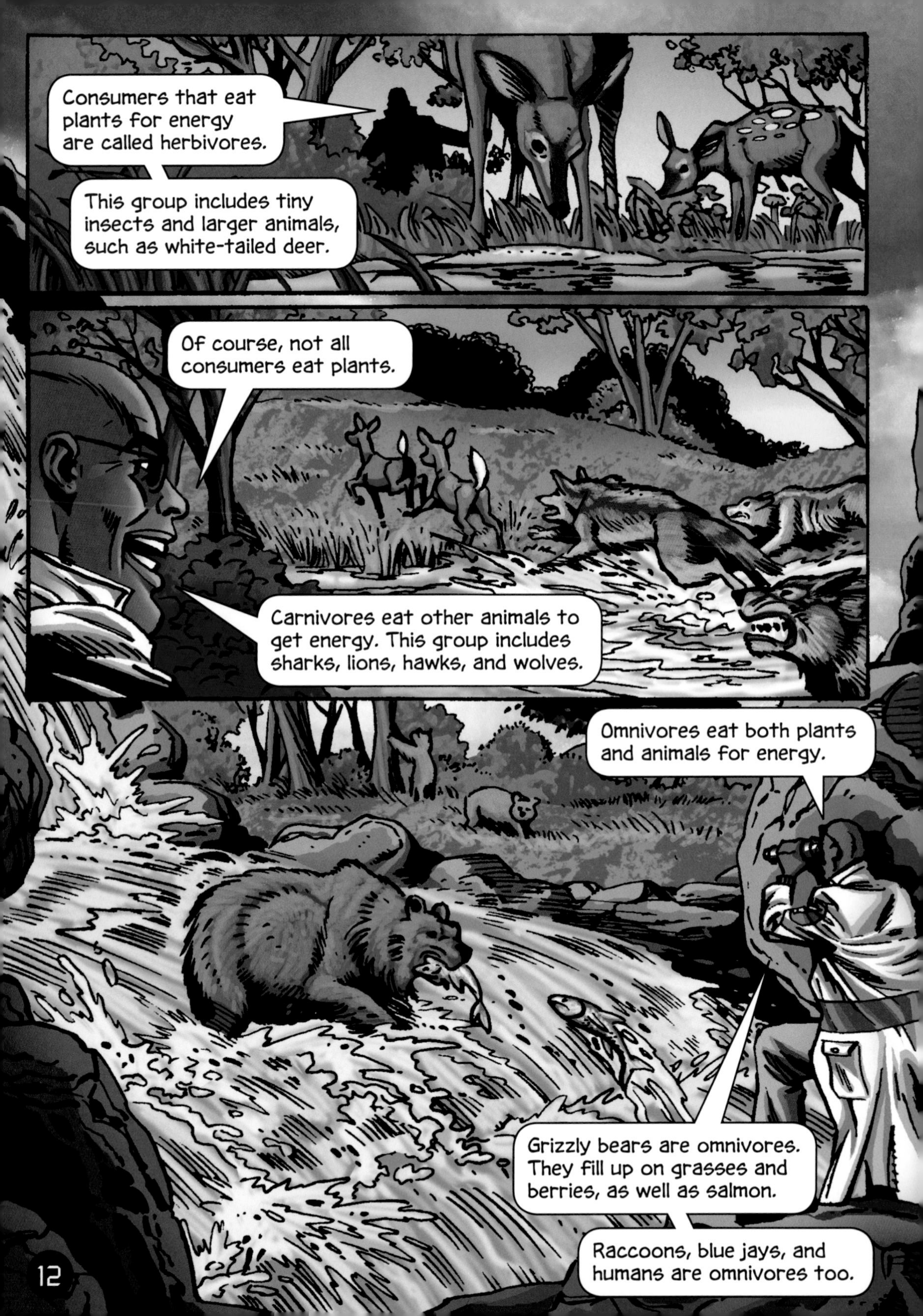

Consumers that eat plants for energy are called herbivores.
This group includes tiny insects and larger animals, such as white-tailed deer.
Of course, not all consumers eat plants.
Carnivores eat other animals to get energy. This group includes sharks, lions, hawks, and wolves.
Omnivores eat both plants and animals for energy.
Grizzly bears are omnivores. They fill up on grasses and berries, as well as salmon.
Raccoons, blue jays, and humans are omnivores too.

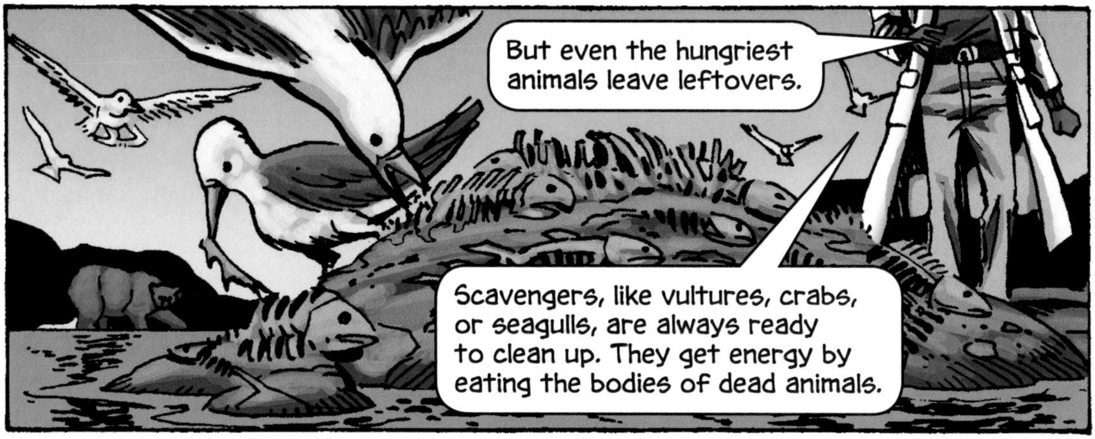
But even the hungriest animals leave leftovers.
Scavengers, like vultures, crabs, or seagulls, are always ready to clean up. They get energy by eating the bodies of dead animals.

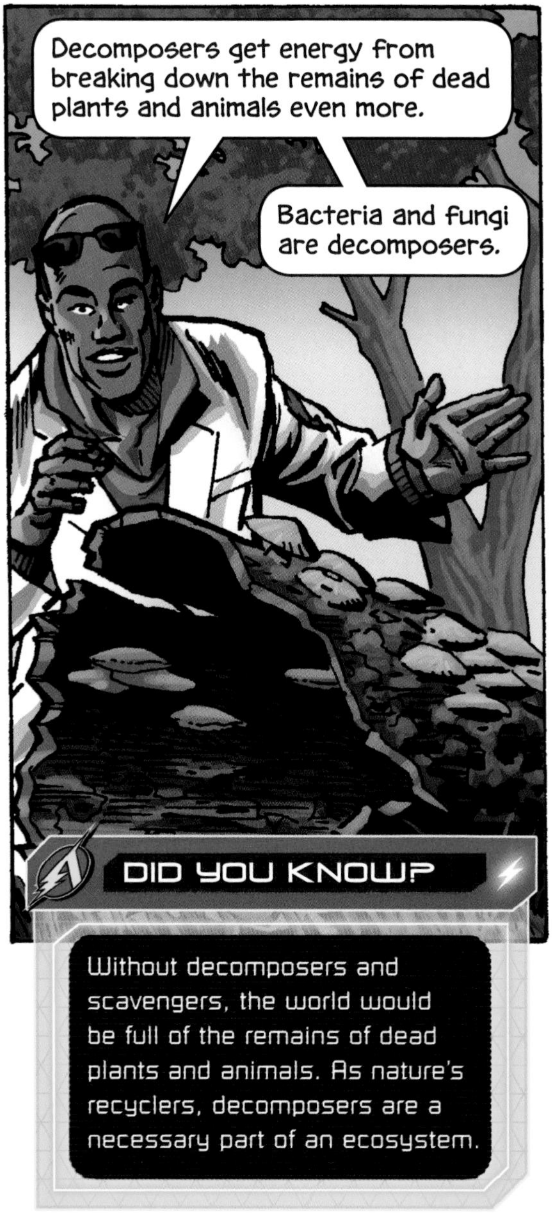
Decomposers get energy from breaking down the remains of dead plants and animals even more.
Bacteria and fungi are decomposers.

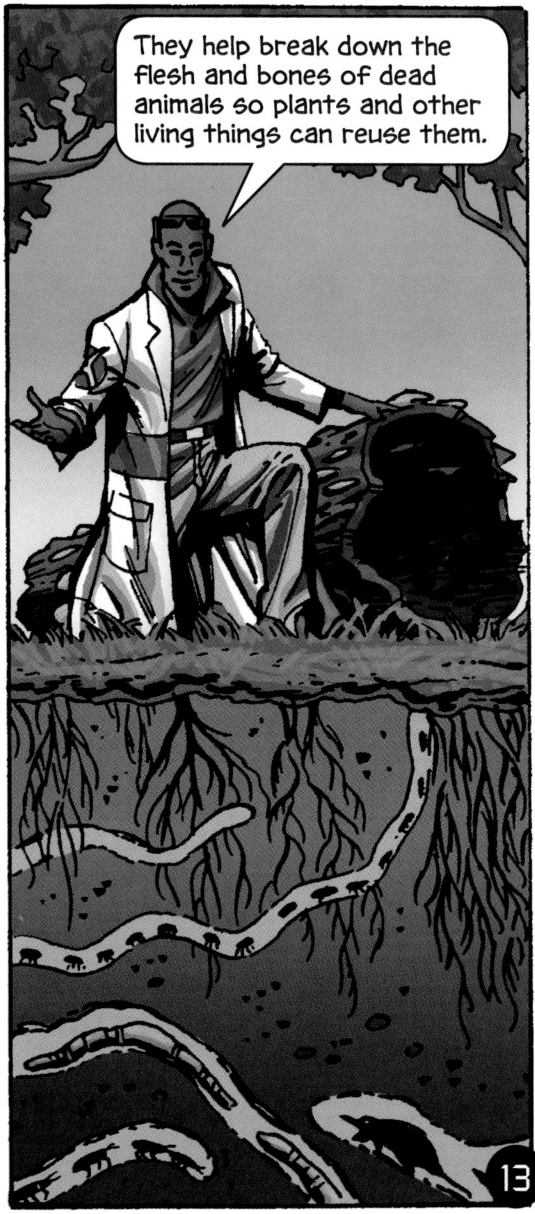
They help break down the flesh and bones of dead animals so plants and other living things can reuse them.

DID YOU KNOW?

Without decomposers and scavengers, the world would be full of the remains of dead plants and animals. As nature's recyclers, decomposers are a necessary part of an ecosystem.

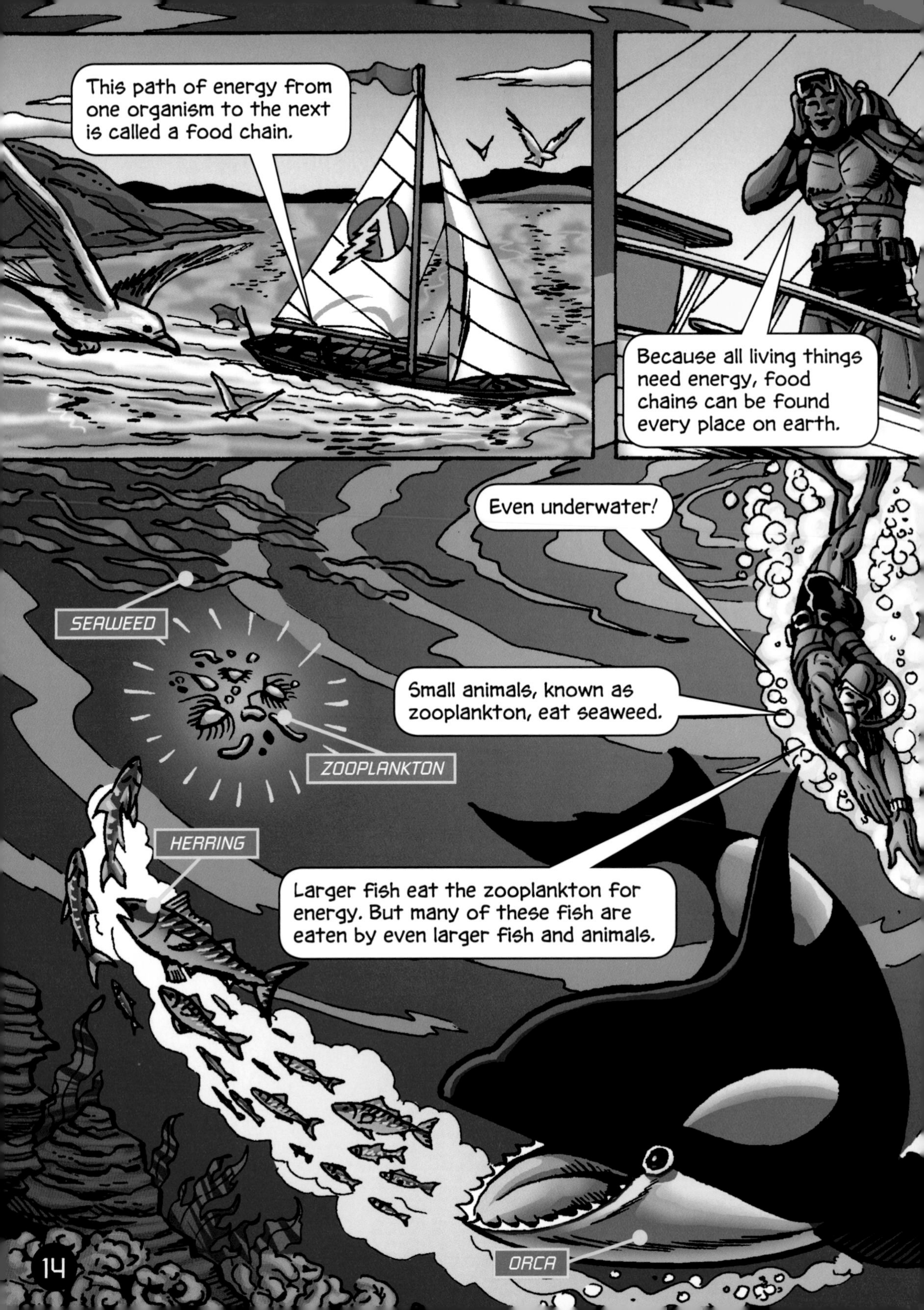
This path of energy from one organism to the next is called a food chain.
Because all living things need energy, food chains can be found every place on earth.
Even underwater!
SEAWEED
Small animals, known as zooplankton, eat seaweed.
ZOOPLANKTON
HERRING
Larger fish eat the zooplankton for energy. But many of these fish are eaten by even larger fish and animals.
ORCA
14

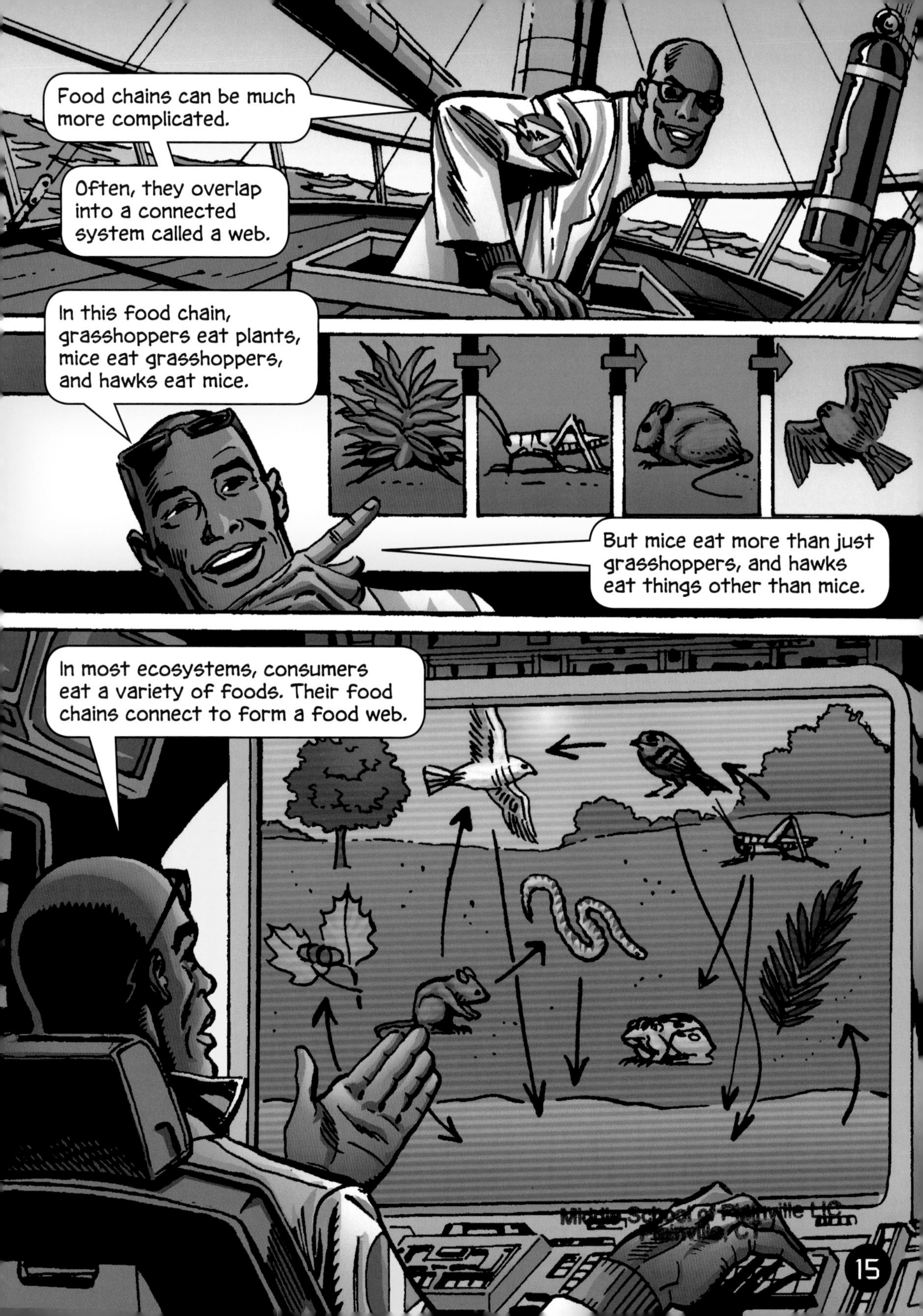
Food chains can be much more complicated.
Often, they overlap into a connected system called a web.
In this food chain, grasshoppers eat plants, mice eat grasshoppers, and hawks eat mice.
But mice eat more than just grasshoppers, and hawks eat things other than mice.
In most ecosystems, consumers eat a variety of foods. Their food chains connect to form a food web.

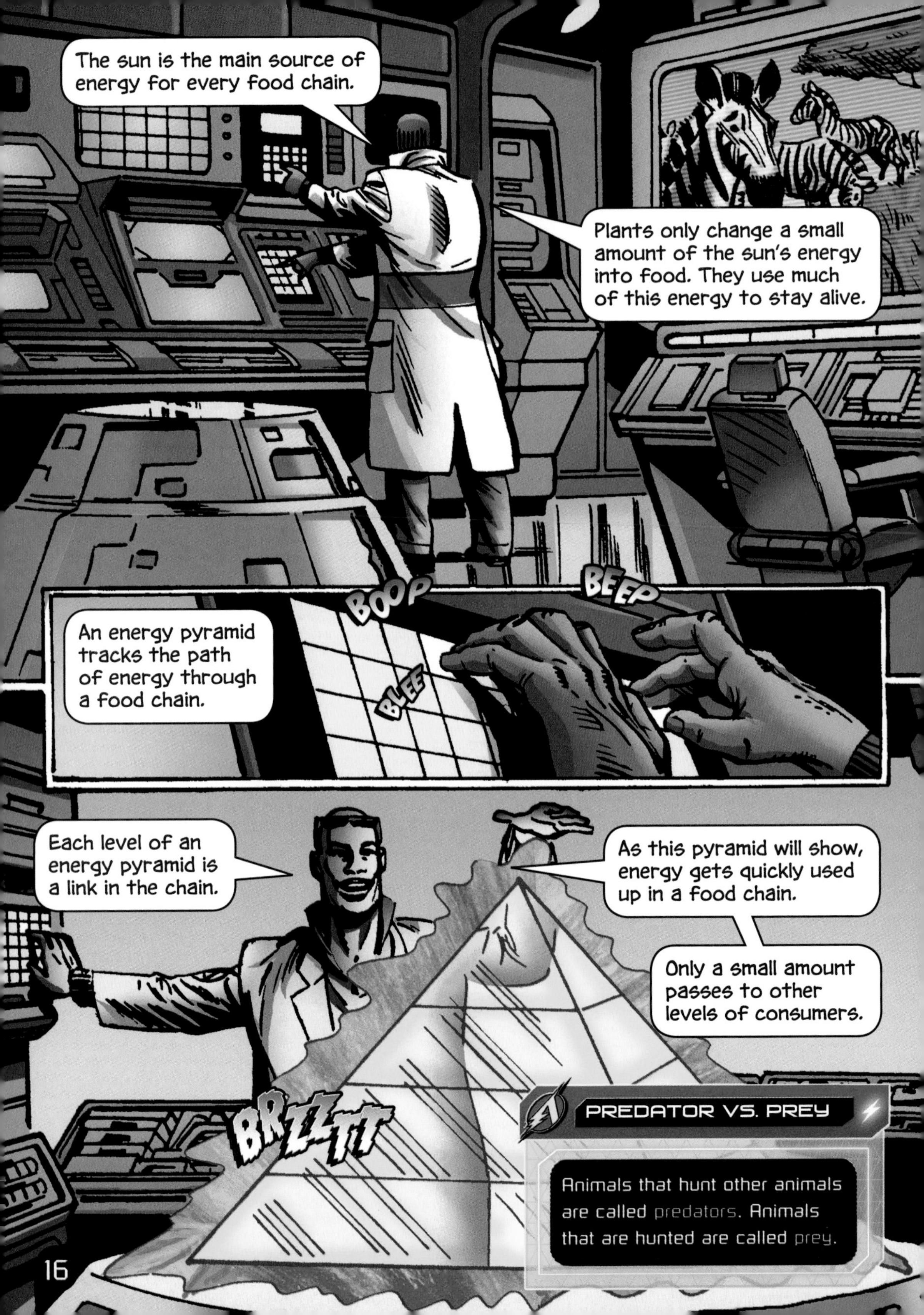
The sun is the main source of energy for every food chain.
Plants only change a small amount of the sun's energy into food. They use much of this energy to stay alive.
BOOP
BEEP
An energy pyramid tracks the path of energy through a food chain.
BLEEE
Each level of an energy pyramid is a link in the chain.
As this pyramid will show, energy gets quickly used up in a food chain.
Only a small amount passes to other levels of consumers.
BRZZZTT

PREDATOR VS. PREY

Animals that hunt other animals are called predators. Animals that are hunted are called prey.

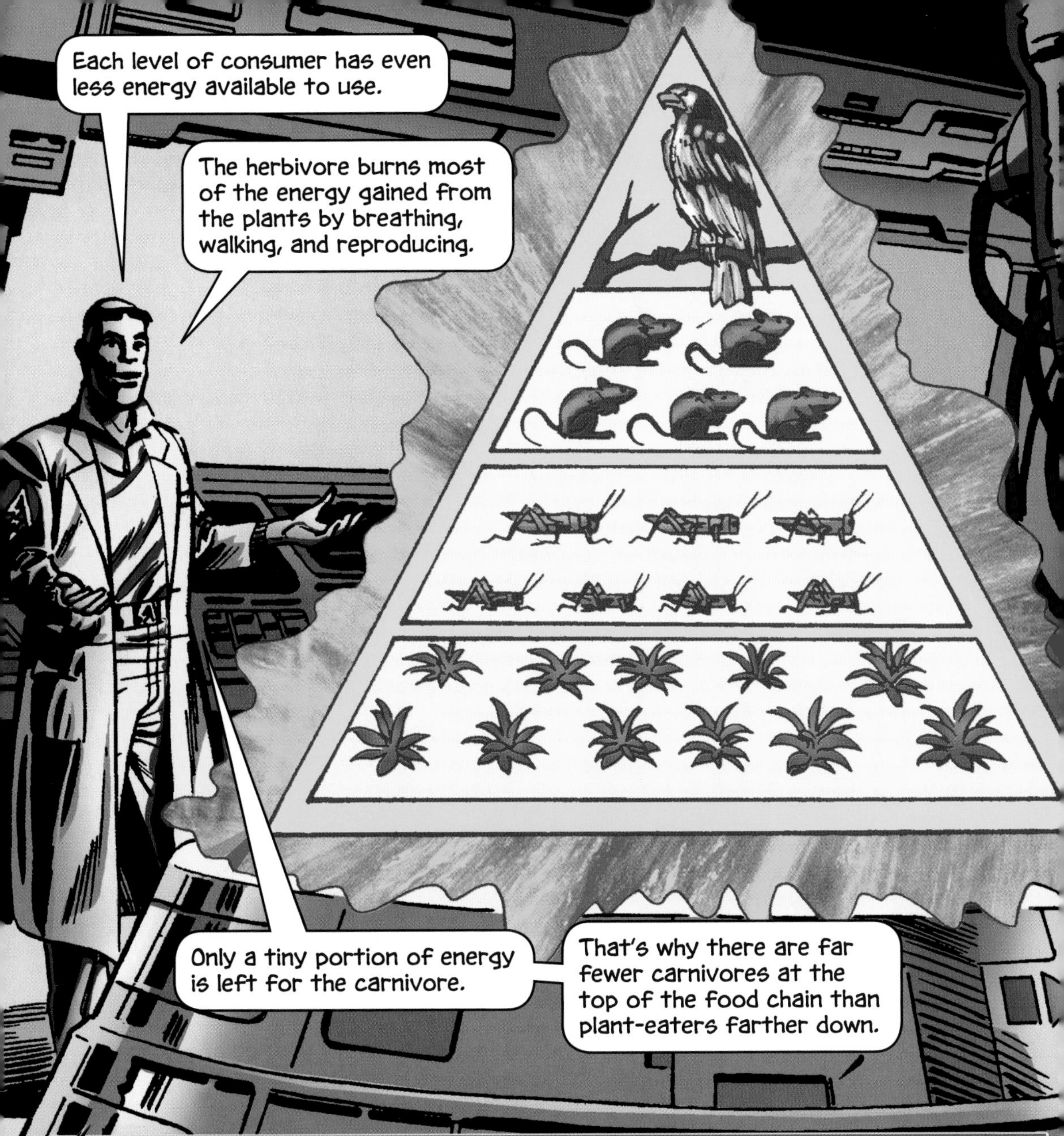
Each level of consumer has even less energy available to use.
The herbivore burns most of the energy gained from the plants by breathing, walking, and reproducing.
Only a tiny portion of energy is left for the carnivore.
That's why there are far fewer carnivores at the top of the food chain than plant-eaters farther down.

PYRAMID OF THE SERENGETI

ACCESS GRANTED: MAX AXIOM

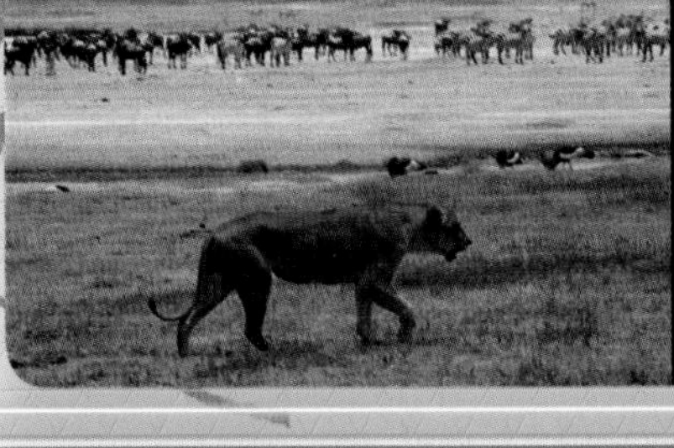

Five square miles in the Serengeti produces about 7,500 tons of grass. These plants can support about 350 gazelles, zebras, and wildebeest. All these animals support one lion. The population of prey and predator stays in balance with these numbers. If there were more lions in the area, they would kill too many plant-eaters and run out of food.

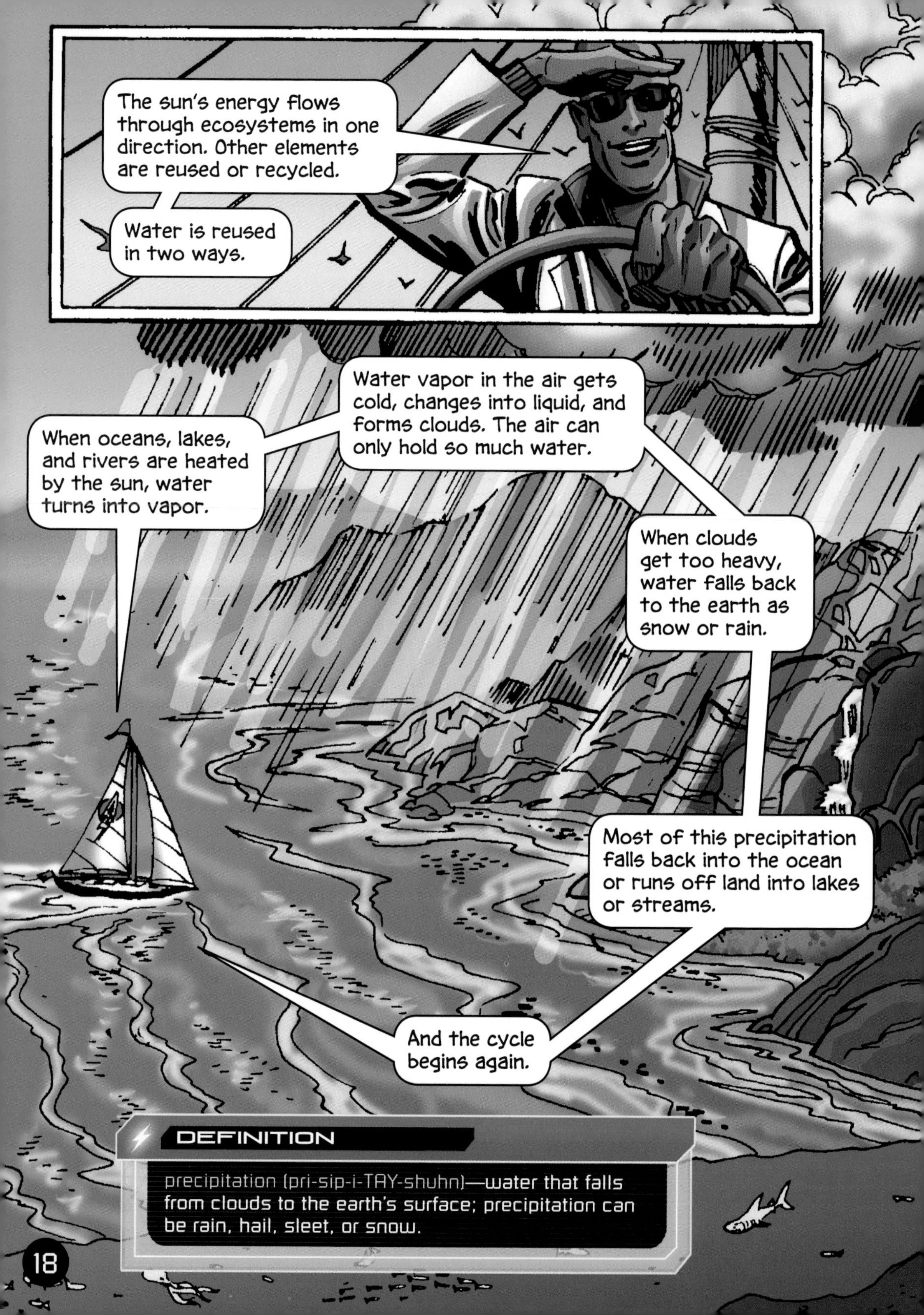
The sun's energy flows through ecosystems in one direction. Other elements are reused or recycled.
Water is reused in two ways.
When oceans, lakes, and rivers are heated by the sun, water turns into vapor.
Water vapor in the air gets cold, changes into liquid, and forms clouds. The air can only hold so much water.
When clouds get too heavy, water falls back to the earth as snow or rain.
Most of this precipitation falls back into the ocean or runs off land into lakes or streams.
And the cycle begins again.

DEFINITION

precipitation (pri-sip-i-TAY-shuhn)—water that falls from clouds to the earth's surface; precipitation can be rain, hail, sleet, or snow.

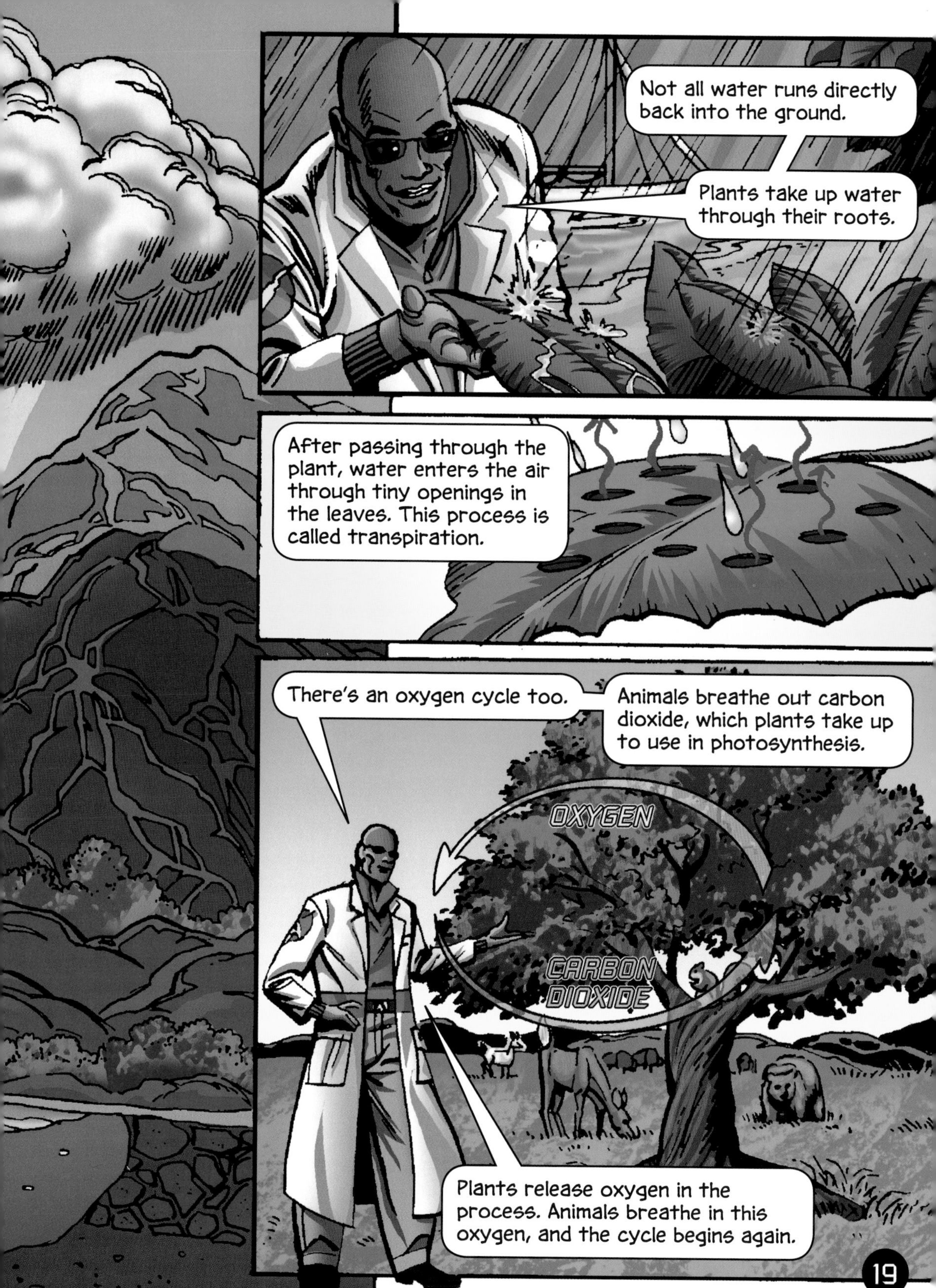

Not all water runs directly back into the ground.
Plants take up water through their roots.
After passing through the plant, water enters the air through tiny openings in the leaves. This process is called transpiration.
There's an oxygen cycle too.
Animals breathe out carbon dioxide, which plants take up to use in photosynthesis.
OXYGEN
CARBON DIOXIDE
Plants release oxygen in the process. Animals breathe in this oxygen, and the cycle begins again.

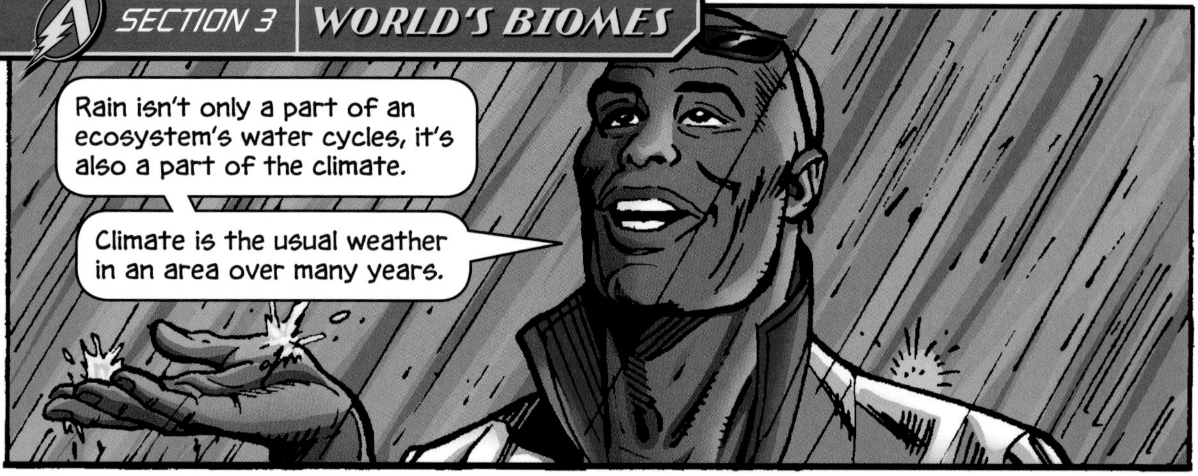
Rain isn't only a part of an ecosystem's water cycles, it's also a part of the climate.
Climate is the usual weather in an area over many years.

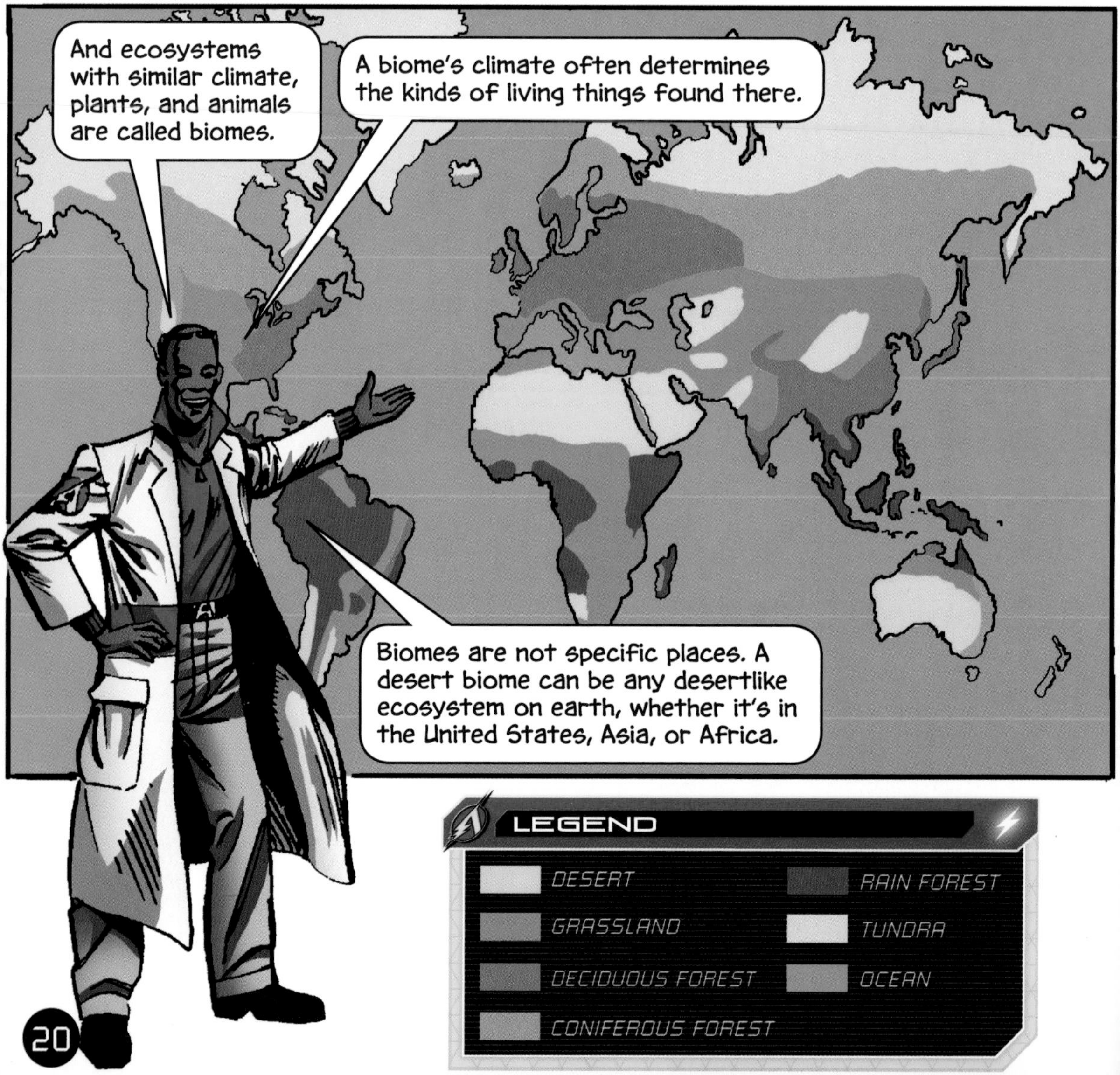
And ecosystems with similar climate, plants, and animals are called biomes.
A biome's climate often determines the kinds of living things found there.
Biomes are not specific places. A desert biome can be any desertlike ecosystem on earth, whether it's in the United States, Asia, or Africa.
LEGEND
DESERT
GRASSLAND
DECIDUOUS FOREST
CONIFEROUS FOREST
RAIN FOREST
TUNDRA
OCEAN

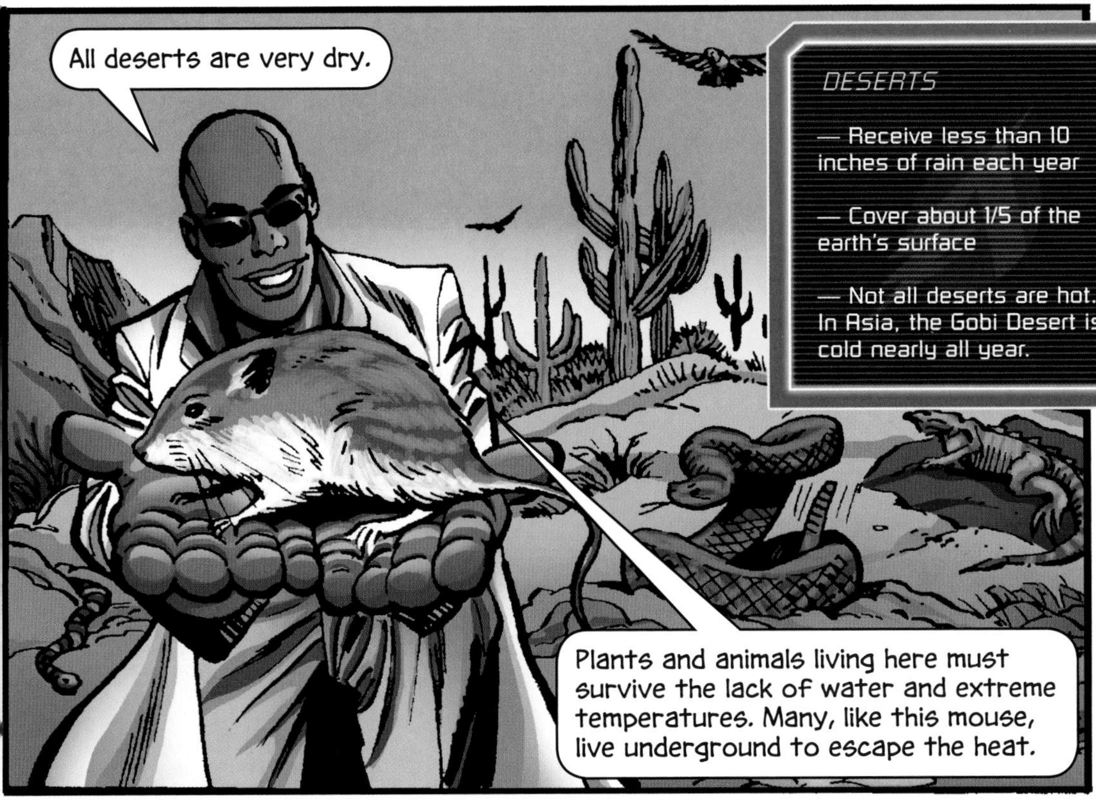
All deserts are very dry.
DESERTS
— Receive less than 10 inches of rain each year
— Cover about 1/5 of the earth's surface
— Not all deserts are hot. In Asia, the Gobi Desert is cold nearly all year.
Plants and animals living here must survive the lack of water and extreme temperatures. Many, like this mouse, live underground to escape the heat.

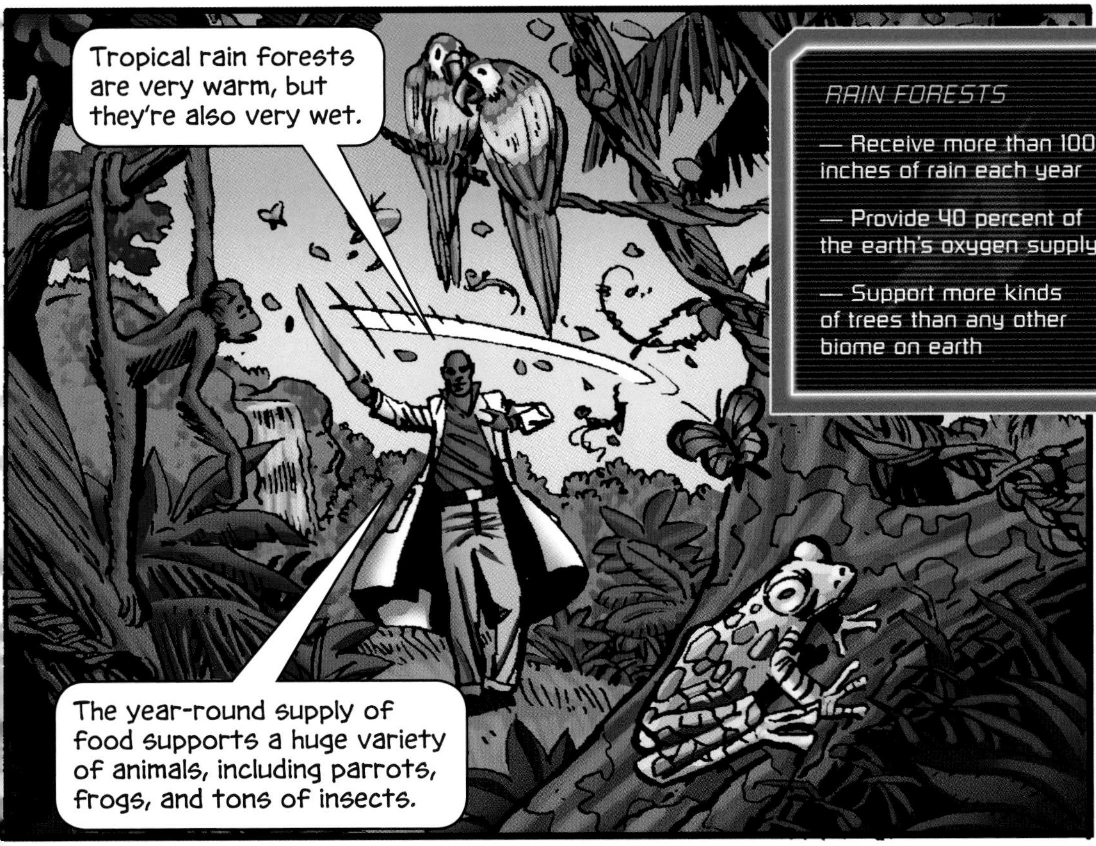
Tropical rain forests are very warm, but they're also very wet.
RAIN FORESTS
— Receive more than 100 inches of rain each year
— Provide 40 percent of the earth's oxygen supply
— Support more kinds of trees than any other biome on earth
The year-round supply of food supports a huge variety of animals, including parrots, frogs, and tons of insects.

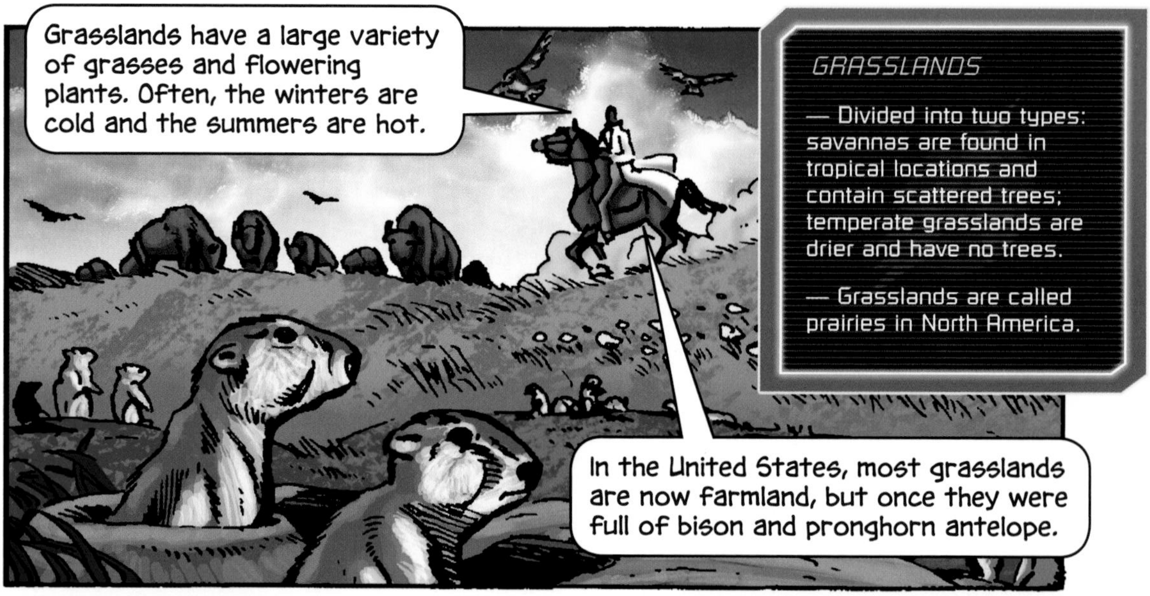
Grasslands have a large variety of grasses and flowering plants. Often, the winters are cold and the summers are hot.
GRASSLANDS
— Divided into two types: savannas are found in tropical locations and contain scattered trees; temperate grasslands are drier and have no trees.
— Grasslands are called prairies in North America.
In the United States, most grasslands are now farmland, but once they were full of bison and pronghorn antelope.

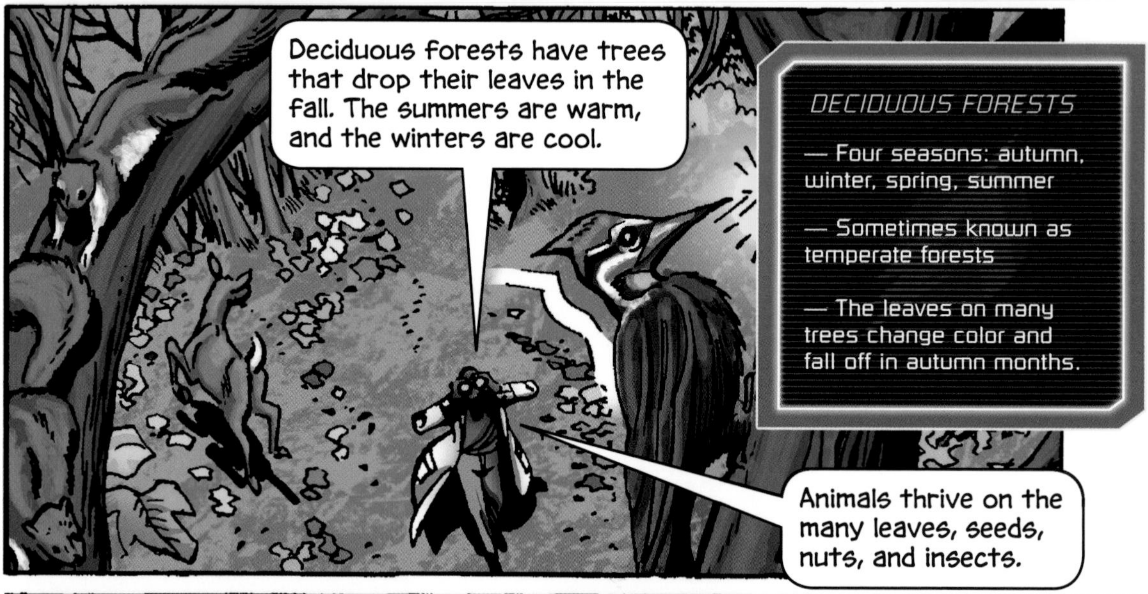
Deciduous forests have trees that drop their leaves in the fall. The summers are warm, and the winters are cool.
DECIDUOUS FORESTS
— Four seasons: autumn, winter, spring, summer
— Sometimes known as temperate forests
— The leaves on many trees change color and fall off in autumn months.
Animals thrive on the many leaves, seeds, nuts, and insects.

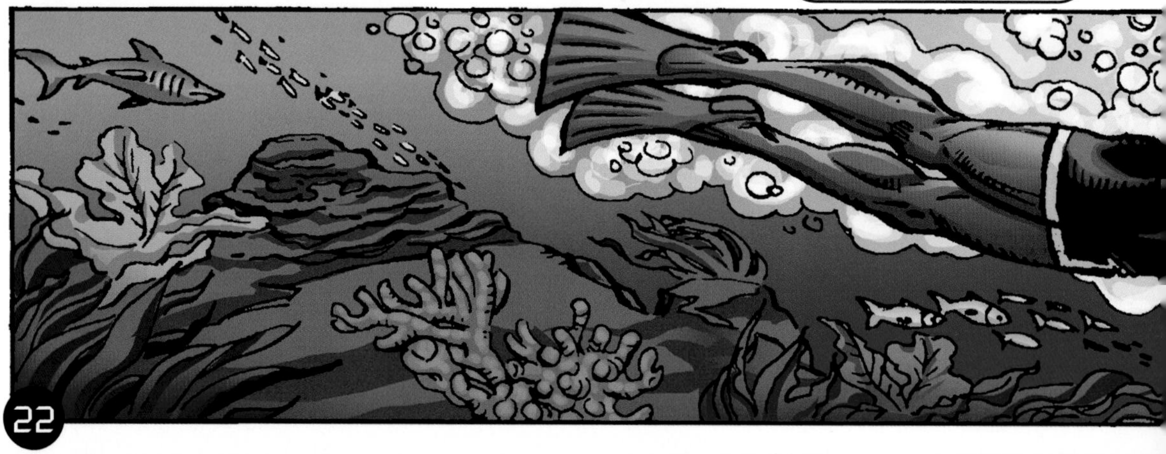

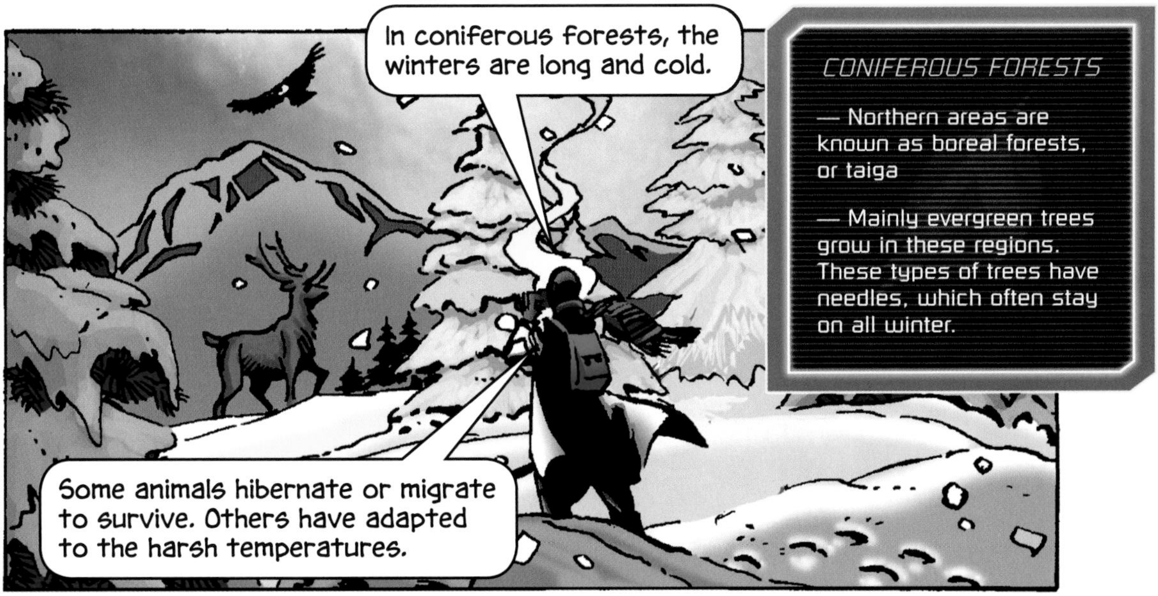
In coniferous forests, the winters are long and cold.
Some animals hibernate or migrate to survive. Others have adapted to the harsh temperatures.
CONIFEROUS FORESTS
— Northern areas are known as boreal forests, or taiga
— Mainly evergreen trees grow in these regions. These types of trees have needles, which often stay on all winter.

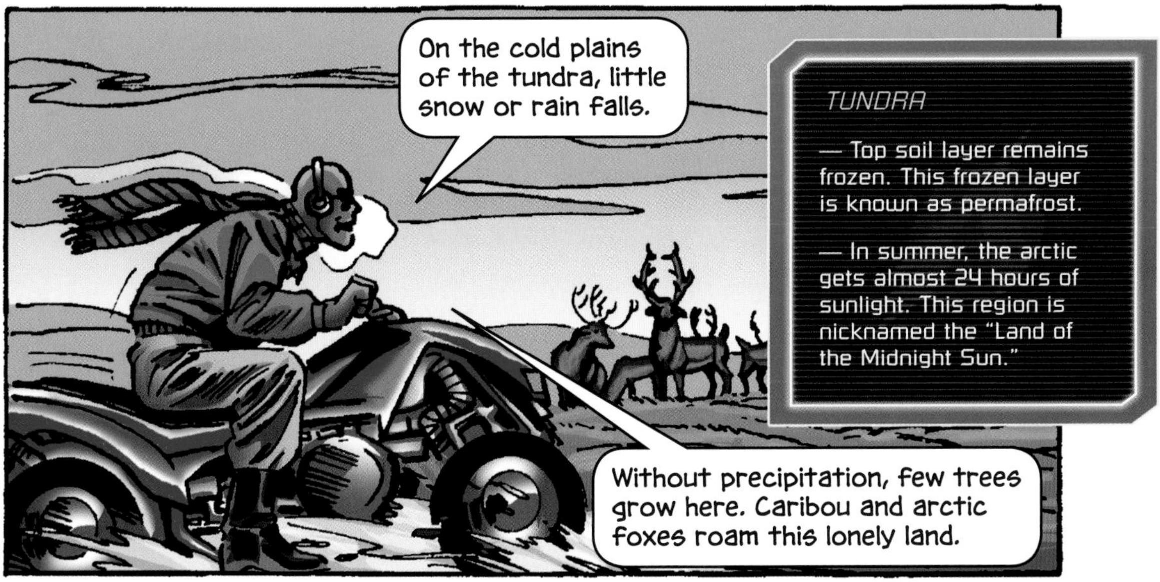
On the cold plains of the tundra, little snow or rain falls.
Without precipitation, few trees grow here. Caribou and arctic foxes roam this lonely land.
TUNDRA
— Top soil layer remains frozen. This frozen layer is known as permafrost.
— In summer, the arctic gets almost 24 hours of sunlight. This region is nicknamed the "Land of the Midnight Sun."

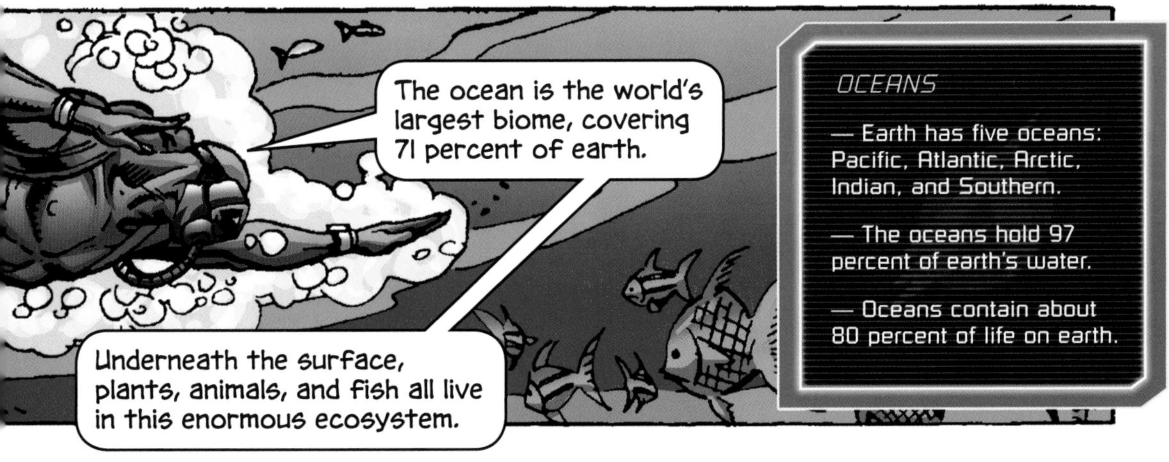
The ocean is the world's largest biome, covering 71 percent of earth.
Underneath the surface, plants, animals, and fish all live in this enormous ecosystem.
OCEANS
— Earth has five oceans: Pacific, Atlantic, Arctic, Indian, and Southern.
— The oceans hold 97 percent of earth's water.
— Oceans contain about 80 percent of life on earth.

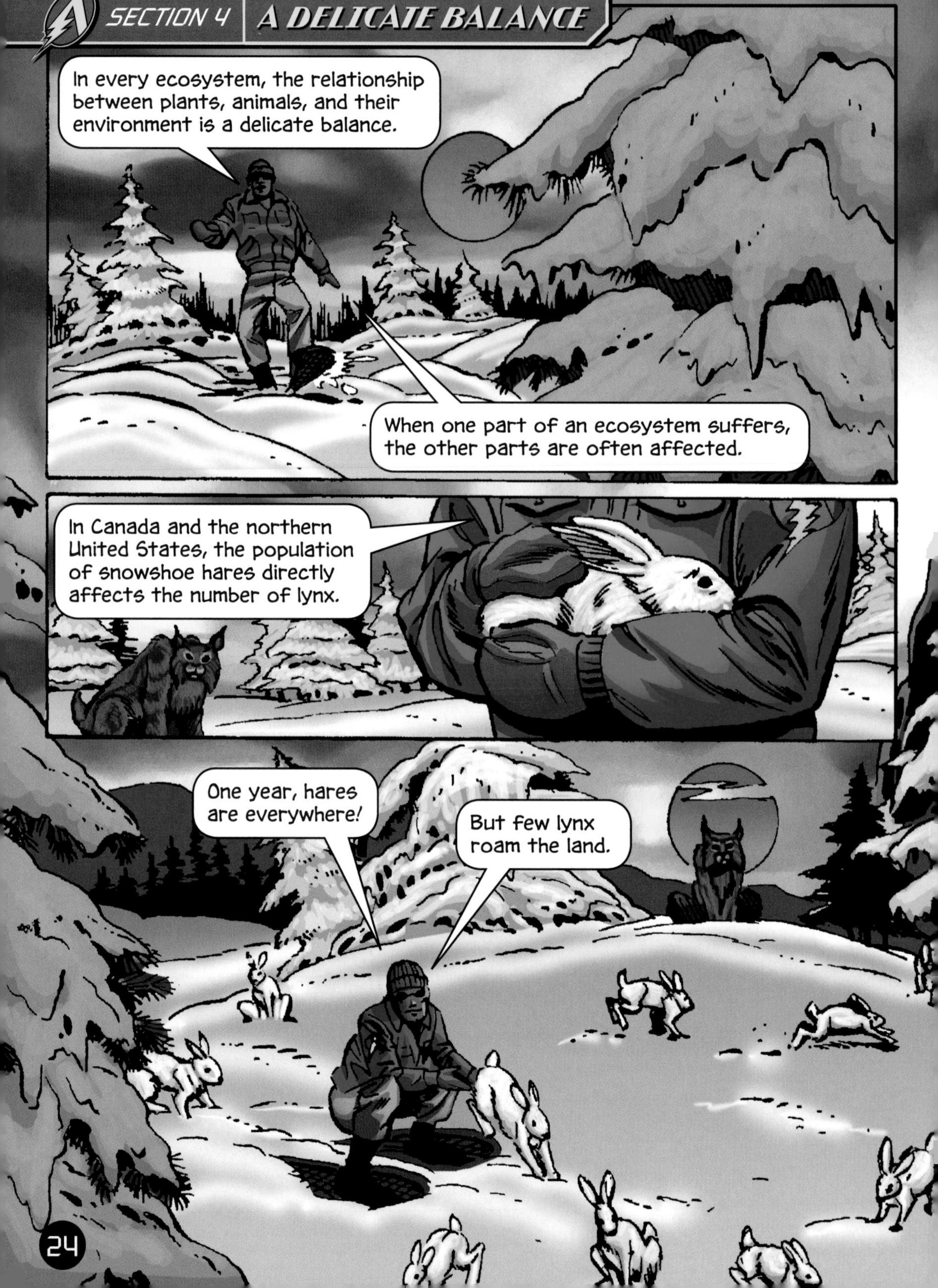
In every ecosystem, the relationship between plants, animals, and their environment is a delicate balance.
When one part of an ecosystem suffers, the other parts are often affected.
In Canada and the northern United States, the population of snowshoe hares directly affects the number of lynx.
One year, hares are everywhere!
But few lynx roam the land.

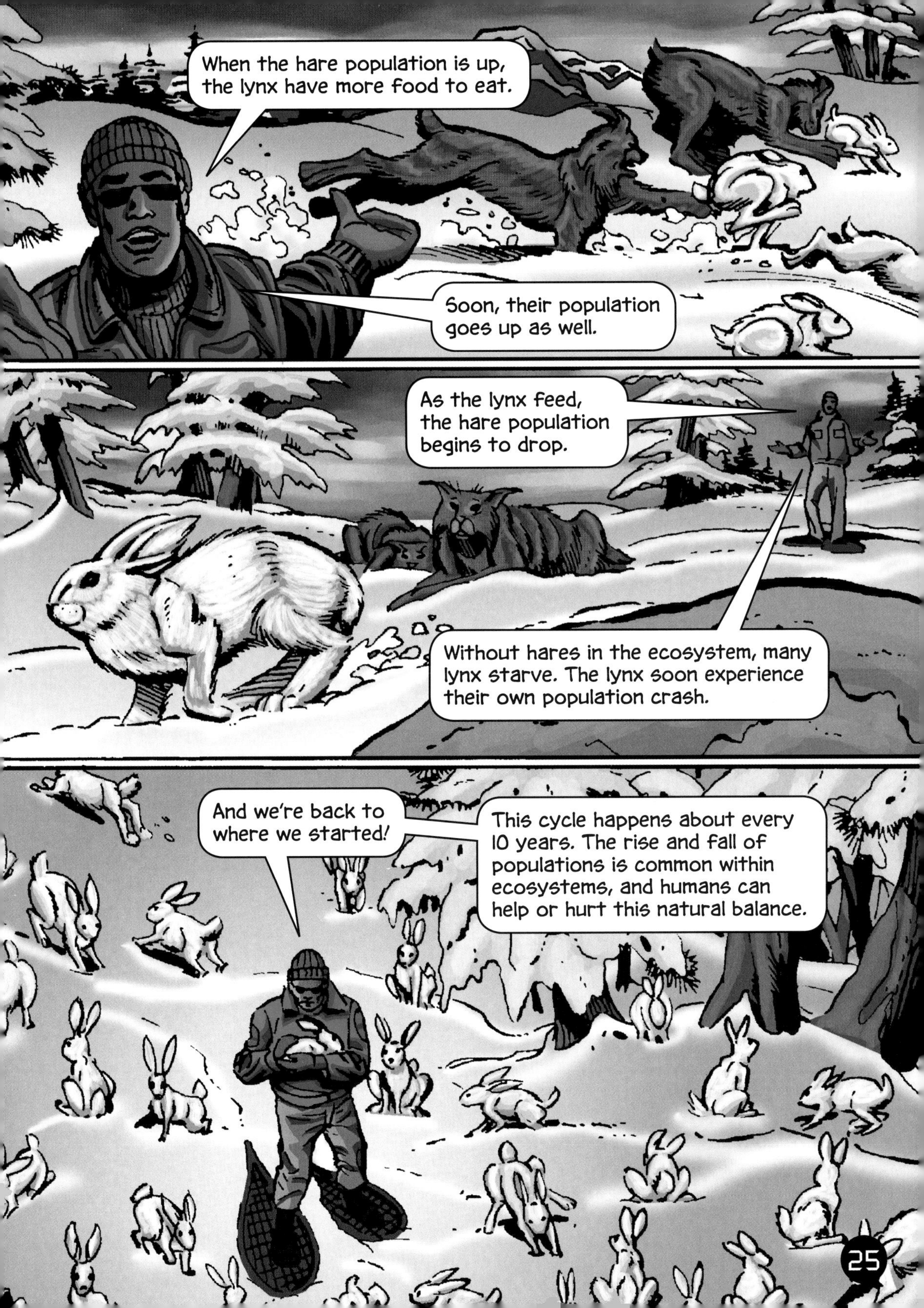
When the hare population is up, the lynx have more food to eat.
Soon, their population goes up as well.
As the lynx feed, the hare population begins to drop.
Without hares in the ecosystem, many lynx starve. The lynx soon experience their own population crash.
And we're back to where we started!
This cycle happens about every 10 years. The rise and fall of populations is common within ecosystems, and humans can help or hurt this natural balance.

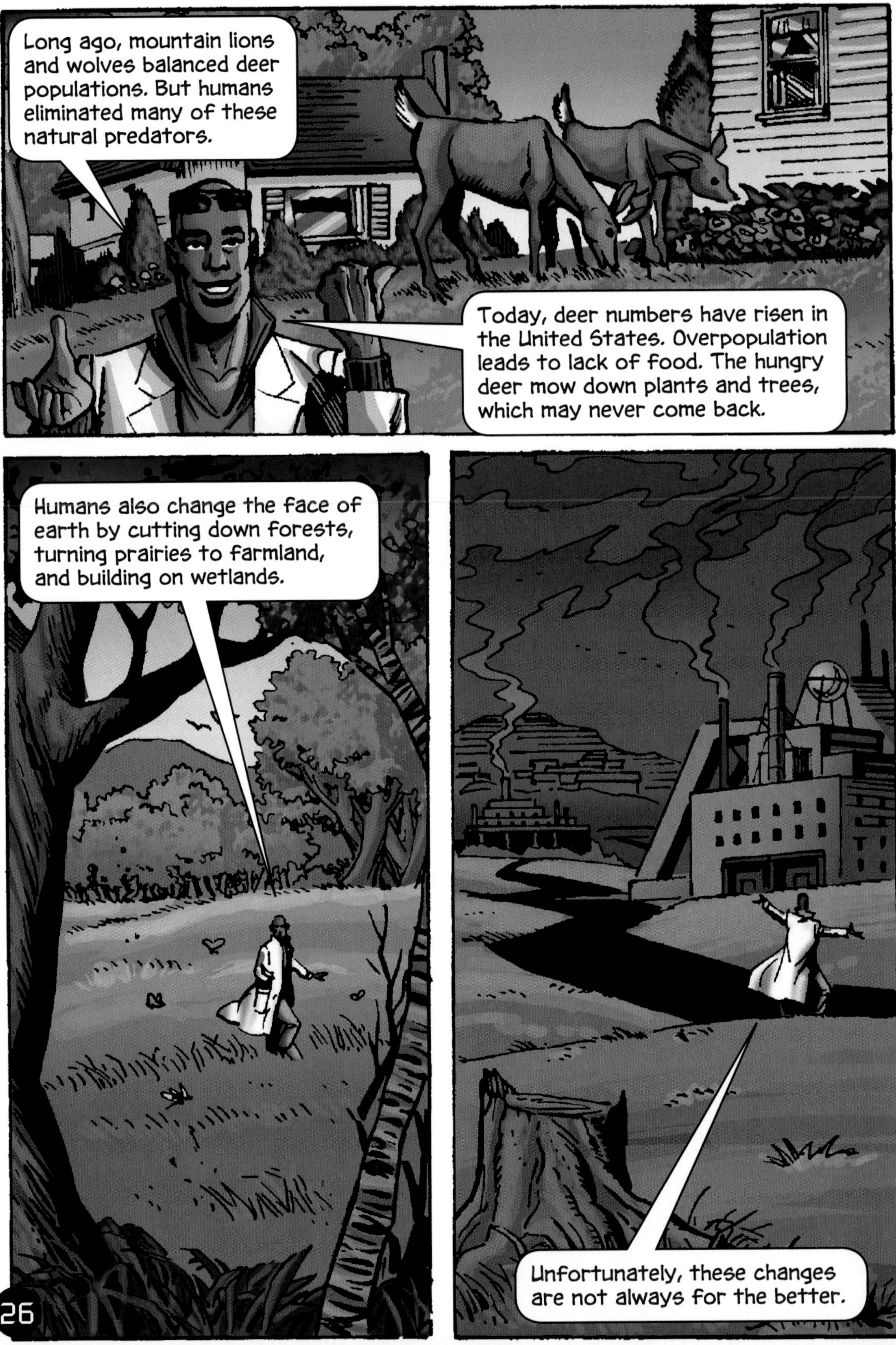

Long ago, mountain lions and wolves balanced deer populations. But humans eliminated many of these natural predators.
Today, deer numbers have risen in the United States. Overpopulation leads to lack of food. The hungry deer mow down plants and trees, which may never come back.
Humans also change the face of earth by cutting down forests, turning prairies to farmland, and building on wetlands.
Unfortunately, these changes are not always for the better.

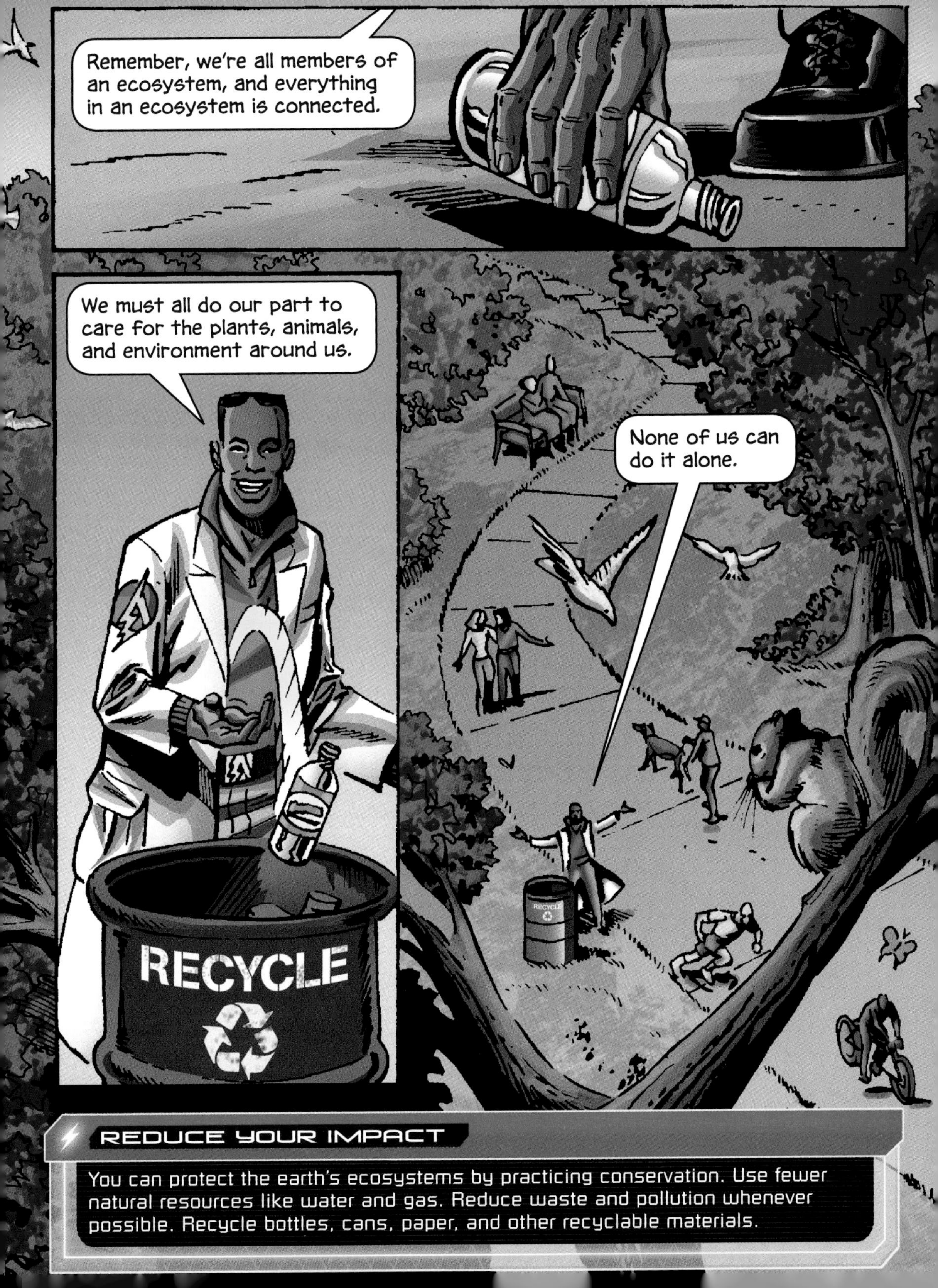
Remember, we're all members of an ecosystem, and everything in an ecosystem is connected.
We must all do our part to care for the plants, animals, and environment around us.
None of us can do it alone.
RECYCLE
RECYCLE

REDUCE YOUR IMPACT

You can protect the earth's ecosystems by practicing conservation. Use fewer natural resources like water and gas. Reduce waste and pollution whenever possible. Recycle bottles, cans, paper, and other recyclable materials.

ECOSYSTEMS

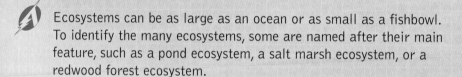

Ecosystems can be as large as an ocean or as small as a fishbowl. To identify the many ecosystems, some are named after their main feature, such as a pond ecosystem, a salt marsh ecosystem, or a redwood forest ecosystem.

Ecosystems are fragile, and alien invasive species can be a major problem. These plants and animals have been introduced to a part of the world where they don't belong. The brown tree snake was originally from Australia and Indonesia. Somehow, this sneaky reptile slithered onto a plane and hitched a ride to the island of Guam. With few predators on Guam, the tree snake has nearly wiped out native forest birds.

Believe it or not, the extinct passenger pigeon was once among the most numerous animals on earth. In the early 1800s, the passenger pigeon population was estimated at 1 to 5 billion birds. Huge, migrating flocks actually darkened the sky when they passed. Largely due to overhunting, the pigeons began to decline. By the 1890s, only small flocks were left. The last passenger pigeon, named Martha, died in the Cincinnati Zoo in 1914.

In the early 1990s, scientists tried to reproduce the ecosystems of earth inside a 3.5-acre (1.4-hectare) building called Biosphere 2. Located near Tucson, Arizona, the building contained a desert, a rain forest, and even a 900,000-gallon (3,406,860-liter) ocean. Some scientists believed buildings like Biosphere 2 could support life on the Moon or Mars. But after only two disappointing missions inside, the experiments ended. Today, visitors can tour the building and learn more about earth's fragile ecosystems.

The rain forest is one of the largest biomes on earth. Sadly, more than 1.5 acres (.6 hectare) of rain forest are destroyed every second.

 People should do their part every day to protect the environment. Several holidays throughout the year help keep us from forgetting this important task:

Earth Day (April 22)—celebrates clean air, land, and water

World Environment Day (June 5)—encourages environmental awareness worldwide

Arbor Day (different in each state)—promotes tree planting

MORE ABOUT

SUPER SCIENTIST

Real name: Maxwell J. Axiom
Hometown: Seattle, Washington
Height: 6' 1"   **Weight:** 192 lbs
Eyes: Brown   **Hair:** None

Super capabilities: Super intelligence; able to shrink to the size of an atom; sunglasses give x-ray vision; lab coat allows for travel through time and space.

Origin: Since birth, Max Axiom seemed destined for greatness. His mother, a marine biologist, taught her son about the mysteries of the sea. His father, a nuclear physicist and volunteer park ranger, schooled Max on the wonders of earth and sky.

One day on a wilderness hike, a megacharged lightning bolt struck Max with blinding fury. When he awoke, Max discovered a newfound energy and set out to learn as much about science as possible. He traveled the globe earning degrees in every aspect of the field. Upon his return, he was ready to share his knowledge and new identity with the world. He had become Max Axiom, Super Scientist.

GLOSSARY

carbon dioxide (KAHR-buhn dye-AHK-side)—a colorless, odorless gas that people and animals breathe out

community (kuh-MYOO-nuh-tee)—populations of people, plants, or animals that live together in the same area and depend on each other

ecology (ee-KOL-uh-jee)—the study of the relationships between plants and animals in their environments

environment (en-VYE-ruhn-muhnt)—the natural world of the land, water, and air

mate (MATE)—to join together for breeding

offspring (OFF-spring)—animals born to a set of parents

organism (OR-guh-niz-uhm)—a living plant or animal

population (pop-yuh-LAY-shuhn)—a group of people, animals, or plants living in a certain place

recycle (ree-SYE-kuhl)—the process of turning something old into something new

transpiration (transs-puh-RAY-shuhn)—the process by which plants give off moisture into the atmosphere

READ MORE

Harman, Rebecca. *Carbon-Oxygen and Nitrogen Cycles.* Earth's Processes. Chicago: Heinemann, 2005.

Juettner, Bonnie. *Photosynthesis.* The KidHaven Science Library. Detroit: KidHaven Press, 2005.

Kalman, Bobbie. *Food Chains and You.* Food Chains Series. New York: Crabtree, 2005.

Petersen, Christine. *Conservation.* A True Book. New York: Children's Press, 2004.

Spilsbury, Louise, and Richard Spilsbury. *The War in Your Backyard: Life in an Ecosystem.* Chicago: Raintree, 2006.

INTERNET SITES

FactHound offers a safe, fun way to find Internet sites related to this book. All of the sites on FactHound have been researched by our staff.

Here's how:
1. Visit *www.facthound.com*
2. Choose your grade level.
3. Type in this book ID **0736868429** for age-appropriate sites. You may also browse subjects by clicking on letters, or by clicking on pictures and words.
4. Click on the **Fetch It** button.

FactHound will fetch the best sites for you!

INDEX

animals
    carnivores, 12, 17
    herbivores, 12, 17
    omnivores, 12
    populations, 8–9, 17,
       24–25, 26, 28
    predators, 16, 17, 26, 28
    prey, 16, 17
    scavengers, 13

biomes, 20–23, 29
    coniferous forests, 20, 23
    deciduous forests, 20, 22
    deserts, 20, 21, 28
    grasslands, 20, 22
    oceans, 18, 23, 28
    rain forests, 20, 21, 28, 29
    tundra, 20, 23
Biosphere 2, 28

climates, 20
conservation, 27

energy, 6, 10, 11, 12, 13, 14,
    16, 17, 18
energy pyramids, 16–17
environment, 4, 7, 9, 24,
    27, 29

food chains, 14–15, 16, 17
    consumers, 10, 11, 12, 15,
      16, 17
    decomposers, 10, 13
    producers, 10, 11
food webs, 15

glucose, 10

nutrients, 11

organisms, 5, 6, 7, 8, 10,
    11, 14
oxygen cycle, 19

photosynthesis, 10, 19
plants, 6, 7, 10, 11, 12, 13,
    14, 15, 16, 17, 19, 20, 21,
    22, 23, 24, 26, 27, 28

recycling, 13, 18, 27

species, 8, 28

water cycle, 18–19, 20
    precipitation, 18, 23
    transpiration, 19
    vapor, 18

Middle School of Plainville LIC
Plainville, CT